The Complete Guide to Lesson Planning and Preparation

ANTHONY HAYNES

continuum

Continuum International Publishing Group
The Tower Building   80 Maiden Lane
11 York Road   Suite 704
London SE1 7NX   New York, NY 10038

www.continuumbooks.com

British Library Cataloguing-in-Publication Data
A catalogue record for this book is available from the British Library.

ISBN: 9781847060709 (paperback)

Library of Congress Cataloging-in-Publication Data
Haynes, Anthony.
Complete guide to lesson planning and preparation / Anthony Haynes.
p. cm.
Includes bibliographical references and index.
ISBN 978-1-84706-070-9 (pbk.)
1. Lesson planning. I. Title.

LB1027.4.H45 2010
371.30281–dc22

Typeset by Newgen Imaging Systems Pvt Ltd, Chennai, India
Printed and bound in Great Britain by
CPI Antony Rowe, Chippenham, Wiltshire

I would like to dedicate this book to the memory of
Michael Marland (1935–2008).

Contents

Contents

Contents

List of figures and tables

Figures

Tables

Acknowledgement

I am grateful to my editor at Continuum, Christina Garbutt, who would seem to be gifted and talented.

1

Teaching as a three-step activity

Teaching may be thought of as a three-step activity. The first step consists of activities – planning and preparation – required before teaching a class; the second of activities in the classroom – classroom management, teaching, learning; and the third of activities that take place after the lesson – assessment, with associated activities such as recording and reporting, and evaluation.

Teachers commonly organize their work according to these three categories: they say things like 'I need to do some preparation now,' 'I'm teaching all day today' or 'I've got to do some marking these evening.' It is the second step – actually being in the classroom, teaching – that usually demands the most energy and produces the emotional highs and lows of the job. That shouldn't, however, divert our attention from the need for thorough professionalism before and after teaching lessons.

The purpose of this book is simply to introduce the thinking required to take the first step – planning and preparation – effectively. It seeks to do this both by outlining a number of fundamental issues and indicating to the reader where further guidance can be found.

The metaphor of teaching as a three-step activity does, however, have some disadvantages. It encourages one to think that the third step – assessment, evaluation and review – is the end of the process. In practice, a good deal of the value of the third step lies in the way it can help the teacher to take the first step – planning and preparation – all over again. In assessing pupils, for example, one learns what's been grasped properly and what one will need to revisit and revise with them next lesson. And by evaluating and reviewing a series of lessons, say, one learns how to improve them next time round.

We should, then, think of the three steps of teaching not so much as the situation shown in Figure 1.1, but rather as that shown in Figure 1.2:

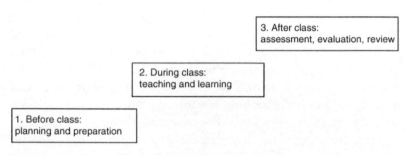

Figure 1.1 The three-step approach

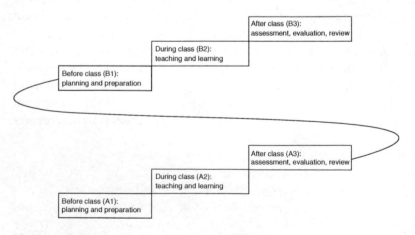

Figure 1.2 The three-step approach as a spiral

Teaching is, then, rather like climbing a spiral staircase. Each flight returns us to the same point – the first step is always planning and preparation – but we begin each flight on a higher level. That is, each time we prepare a lesson we are better informed than we were before. Teaching doesn't always feel like that, of course – sometimes you may feel more like you're going in circles. But I think it's the conviction that one can always move onwards and upwards that keeps teachers going. In truth, the teacher who is perpetually moving in circles probably isn't taking the third step very skilfully.

Our staircase metaphor still isn't quite right, though. Or, rather, the way I've presented it isn't quite right – because so far I've talked about teaching as if it were a linear process: you plan and prepare your lessons, *then* you teach them, *then* you assess and evaluate and review them, *then* you plan and prepare again and so on. In fact, however, teachers need to think in *both* directions – upwards and downwards, as it were – at the same time.

For example, when you're preparing your lessons, you need to be thinking *already* about assessment. You need to be asking yourself questions such as, 'What are the assessment requirements for this course (in terms of, for example, examination syllabuses or government requirements)?' or 'What opportunities for assessment will this lesson produce?' This approach is sometimes known as 'backward design'. In terms of our metaphor, we might say that, when it comes to climbing a staircase, it's usually best to look ahead by considering where that staircase leads to and whether it offers the most efficient route to wherever one wants to go.

Through working at various times with novice teachers I've come to believe that (a) learning to see teaching as a staircase – on which the end of one flight leads directly to the beginning of the next – and (b) learning to think in both directions – both upwards and downwards – are the two most fundamental lessons in teacher development.

Planning and preparation

I find it helpful to visualize the first step of teaching, that is, the planning and preparation stage, as a building – one with four walls and three storeys. The building has four cornerstones providing structure and strength. The cornerstones consist of:

- Educational aims.
- Needs analysis.
- Context.
- The structure of cognition.

The next four chapters below are intended to help teachers put each of these cornerstones in place.

The first of the three storeys is long-term, curricular, planning. This is examined in Chapter 6. The second storey and third storey consist, respectively, of medium- and short-term planning – both outlined in Chapter 7. The third storey contains, as it were, three rooms of particular interest, namely time, space and language – these are explored in Chapters 9, 10 and 11, respectively. Before we come to those chapters, however, there is Chapter 8, which considers educational resources. To continue the building metaphor, resources may be thought of as the windows: they enable our pupils to see the world and provide illumination.

Chapter 12 discusses two concepts that, because they are overarching, may be thought of as providing the roof of the building. They are progression and differentiation.

Chapter 13, the final chapter focuses on assessment. Though at first glance it may seem surprising to include a chapter on this topic, I hope that, in the light of the discussion above, the rationale is clear: as we saw from the analogy of the spiral staircase, though planning and assessment may be at opposite ends of the teaching process, the latter in fact feeds into the former.

Subject teaching

This book is designed for all teachers, regardless of the subjects they teach. This does, however, present a problem. Subject teaching is often the main prism for teachers' thinking about education – and traditions and approaches vary between subjects. To omit altogether a consideration of subject teaching would leave the discussion at a maddeningly abstract level. Discussing each and every subject, on the other hand, would be impractical – and certainly beyond the capability of this (and perhaps any) author.

My solution is to provide a discussion of how one would teach a subject that is, in fact, very rarely taught in schools at all, at least in any sustained way – namely architecture. This might seem a bizarre solution. There is, however, a certain logic to it. Architecture is a wonderfully cross-curricular subject. Architects draw on the disciplines of mathematics, science and engineering in order to, for example, calculate stresses and loads or environmental impacts and to select building materials appropriately. Their decisions over the use of space require an appreciation both of behavioural sciences and of human geography, planning and law. Architecture has its own language (I once inadvertently flummoxed a colleague by referring to the 'clerestory' windows in his classroom) and also its own styles and traditions – my children, for example, attend a school built in 1937 in 'Bauhaus' style. Architecture is, therefore, a subject easier than most for teachers from across the curriculum to relate to. The examples concerning the teaching of architecture are designed, therefore, to show how general ideas look when applied to subject teaching. I invite you to relate these examples to your own experiences of subject teaching – whichever subject area(s) you teach in – through comparison and contrast.

Sources

In preparing this book I've sought to cast my net wide. In the process I have come to appreciate that there are a number of parallel canons on teaching. First and most obviously there are resources aimed at school teachers and trainees. These include practical books, such as the many fine titles by Louisa Leaman, and weightier textbooks by authors such as Andrew Pollard.

Second, there are training resources, aimed at those responsible for human resource development in industry. There are, for example, books like Tom Goad's *The First-Time Trainer* and Peter Taylor's

How to Design a Training Course. There are also many books about coaching and mentoring at work. These 'HR' books are stocked on the business shelves, rather than in the education section of bookshops and libraries, and so rarely find their way into the hands of teachers. This is a shame, because many of them would be useful to teachers. Indeed, such resources tend to be more pragmatic, more concise, less fussy, and less disfigured with educational jargon, than many of those aimed at teachers. In particular, the subjects of needs analysis, stakeholder management and the setting of objectives – discussed in Chapters 2 and 7 – are given more emphasis in the literature of training than in the literature of education.

There are also resources designed to support the world of English Language Teaching (ELT). Some of these are of course specialist – dealing with such topics as the teaching of modal verbs – but many focus on quite general topics and would be of benefit to teachers of other subjects too. In particular, the literature of ELT is rich in guidance on course planning and the development and use of resources.

Finally, there are smaller, though growing, literatures for teachers and lecturers in various sectors (further, higher and adult education) of post-compulsory education. I've taught in each of these sectors, as well as in schools, and found them less different than, I think, their practitioners usually suppose them to be. In writing this book I have, therefore, drawn on resources such as *Teaching in Post-compulsory Education*, edited by Fred Fawbert, and Alastair Irons, *Enhancing Learning through Formative Assessment and Feedback*.

I hope that drawing on advice from the worlds of training, ELT and post-compulsory education, as well as that of school teaching, lends this book a refreshing feel. The main source of guidance, however, has been (along with, inevitably, my own experience of teaching), discussion with numerous teachers, many of whom have been very generous in this regard. This has had the advantage of highlighting a number of issues of importance to teachers but somewhat neglected in the professional literature.

I have outlined above some of the salient features of this book. The most important feature of all, however, is simply that I've tried to 'cut the crap' and tell the truth, as I see it, about teaching.

Further reading

Among the many general texts on teaching, aimed mainly at the beginning teacher, I have selected for the following list one title for each sector. I suggest, however, that whichever sector you may teach in, you may find useful ideas and suggestions in any of these books.

- Mark O'Hara, *Teaching 3–8*, 3rd ed.
- Andrew Pollard, *Reflective Teaching*, 3rd ed.
- Susan Capel et al., *Learning to Teach in the Secondary School*, 4th ed.
- Yvonne Hillier, *Reflective Teaching in Further and Adult Education*, 2nd ed.
- Heather Fry et al., *A Handbook of Teaching & Learning in Higher Education*, 2nd ed.
- Tom Goad, *The First-Time Trainer.*

A book that develops the idea of backward design is Jay McTighe and Grant Wiggins's, *Understanding by Design.*

2

Aims

Before we set about teaching a class, we should surely think carefully about what we're trying to achieve. You may wonder whether I need that 'surely'. Would anyone really suggest that we should*n't* think carefully about what we're trying to achieve? You may even consider my opening assertion so self-evidently true as not to need saying at all. Yet perhaps the idea that we should think carefully about what we are trying to achieve is one of those that most people would agree with but few actually do.

There are reasons for believing so. If, for example, you read the general texts that I recommended in the 'Further reading' section of Chapter 1, you'll find that – good books though they are – they have between them very little to say about the aims of education. And in this they reflect the talk in school staffrooms, where the busy-ness of teaching – the daily round of discussing pupils, finding resources, passing on information and so on – tends to drown out discussions of more long-term concerns.

Even in the more secluded world of teacher education colleges, relatively little attention seems to have been devoted to educational aims. In the preface to his book, *The Aims of Education Restated*, John White noted that there had 'not been as yet any book-length investigation of priorities among educational aims'. White was writing in 1982. It is not very different today, though the 'Further reading' section at the end of this chapter does list some such books published since White was writing.

It is not only the daily business of teaching that crowds out a discussion of educational aims. It is also the profession's suspicion of theory. Discussion that is abstract, discussion that is not couched in terms of the here-and-now, is readily dismissed as overly theoretical ('It's all very well in theory, but I've got thirty kids to teach'). And in some circumstances theory is indeed out of place. When the school fire alarm goes off, one doesn't stop to philosophize.

The problem comes when theory and practice are seen as *necessarily* alien to each other. For a start, that view is inconsistent, since the assumption that theory and practice are mutually exclusive is of course itself a theoretical one. More importantly, we need to remember that theory can often be applied to practice. That is what good professionals do – in teaching, as in other professions such as medicine or law. Indeed, theoretical thinking on the part of the teacher can even on occasion be thought of as a kind of practice itself – and a particularly high-order, powerful, kind of practice at that.

The example of quality management

At this point it is helpful, since this book is concerned above all with quality in education, to draw a comparison with the management of quality in industry. Imagine that you are running a company that manufactures widgets. You set up a production line along which various components are added to the widget as it moves along. At the end of the line, the finished widgets are checked by a quality control department. Those that are found to be sub-standard in some way are discarded. Provided the quality control is rigorous enough, this approach to the management of quality does work, in the sense that it weeds out sub-standard products. But it is also very wasteful. It allows problems to develop and then deals only with the symptoms. Think of all the resources used in making those widgets that get discarded at the end of the process.

Rather than manage quality only at the end of the process, supposing we do so from the very start? Supposing we define what it is we are trying to achieve and then design the system most likely to achieve that end result? This is the starting point for an approach known, in management jargon, as 'Total Quality Management' (TQM). The first move in implementing TQM is always to specify what the point of each business process is and what it is supposed to achieve. This, of course, involves standing back from the production line. That is, the first move is always theoretical.

The jargon ('TQM') and the talk of widgets may make all this sound remote from the school classroom. But a moment's thought will confirm that this approach is in fact *more* pertinent to teaching than it is to the manufacture of widgets. A wasteful system of quality control in the widget industry may be a problem for lots of people – for the managers, the shareholders and the bank – but at least it isn't a problem for the widgets themselves. The same cannot be said of pupils in schools. If their education is not well designed, it is they who suffer. And in most cases they don't get another chance. We need, therefore, to get things right from the start.

TQM provides a good example of how a little theory – standing back from the system, deciding what it is you're trying to achieve and then designing the system accordingly – can in fact be very practical.

Educational aims

So what are our aims in education? What are we teaching *for*? Between them, educators have several different aims. Consider, for example, the following:

1. There are aims concerning progression. The primary school, for example, aims to equip pupils with the skills they will need in secondary education. The secondary school aims to equip pupils with the skills they will need in further study or training.
2. A second type of aim, which may be a subset of (1), is to enable the pupil to achieve formal qualifications. In the independent sector, for example, preparatory schools aim to help pupils succeed in their Common Entrance exams for public school. Secondary schools aim to help students achieve good results in

their diplomas, baccalaureate and so on. Universities aim to help people achieve good degree results and so on.

3. We also aim to equip pupils with an ability to earn a livelihood – to land and hold down a job or perhaps to start their own business.

4. Earning a living is not the only aspect of adult life that schools aim to equip their pupils for. Such aims as teaching pupils how to be effective citizens and how to live healthy lifestyles, manage their finances, raise children and so on are also not uncommon.

5. The above aims are mostly concerned with pupils' futures. In addition, there are aims concerned with the present. Schools often aim to teach pupils the study skills they need for their current courses, to treat each other fairly, to oppose bullying, to say 'No' to drugs and so on.

These aims are primarily concerned with the development of the individual – or at least are couched as such. This is typical of the Western liberal tradition. If you look at the stated aims – in prospectuses, for example – of schools in this tradition, you will see that they typically use phrases such as 'We aim to help each pupil develop to the best of his or her ability.'

(A) Consider your own education. How much weight do you think your teachers gave each of the above aims? How much difference do you think there was between the aims of (i) each institution (school, college, etc.) that you attended and (ii) the teachers within one of institutions that you attended?

(B) How much weight should you give to each of the above aims in your own teaching?

So far we have looked at educational aims in relation to the individual pupil. However, it is also possible to look at them from the point of view of society. A society may wish, for example, to ensure that its heritage is communicated to the next generation. It may wish its young citizens to be well versed in, for example, its historical landmarks, its geography, its customs and traditions.

To some extent, societal aims for education are simply the flip-side of the individual aims. Just as we want the individual pupil to emerge as an employable person, so we want our society to have a skilled workforce. We might want each individual pupil to enjoy a healthy life *and* to help reduce illness among the population as a whole.

We shouldn't conclude, however, that looking at educational aims from the perspectives of the individual or society *always* amounts to the same thing in the end. Sometimes the emphases look very different. A society may want, for example, to convey its heritage to the next generation, not so much for the sake of the individual pupils, but for its own sake. Many social aims are based on a belief that education has a key role to play in preserving continuity and promoting social cohesion.

It helps, therefore, to think of educational aims as falling somewhere on a continuum between the individual, at one end, and the society or community at the other:

Individual ◄─────────────────────► Social

Figure 2.1 The individual/social continuum

What we have said here of societies as a whole may apply equally to particular groups – religious or ethnic communities, say – within the wider society. Often, indeed, the school itself as a community has its own traditions that it is eager to preserve.

> Again, consider your own education. What examples of aims that were primarily social do you think you experienced? On the basis of their educational aims, where on the above continuum (Figure 2.1) would you place each of the institutions that you attended?

Another way of grouping educational aims is according to the extent to which they promote change. The aim of education is sometimes to preserve tradition – to ensure, for example, that our heritage is not lost, that skills are kept alive between generations or that aspects of history are commemorated. School nativity plays at Christmas often function in this way.

On the other hand, education is sometimes seen as an agent of change. For example, in many parts of the world education has been used to introduce new agricultural techniques or ways to combat disease. In the West, enterprise education is becoming more popular. One of its aims is to encourage pupils to think how they could make a difference, for example by starting a new business. And the promotion of critical thinking is often cited as an important aim: educators often argue that it is important for pupils not only to learn about a society's traditions but also to challenge them.

We can, therefore, think of a second continuum running from conservative aims at one end to radical aims at the other:

Conservative ◄————————————► Radical

Figure 2.2 The conservative/radical continuum

Once again, think of the education you have received. To what extent were its aims conservative and to what extent radical? Where on the above continuum (Figure 2.2) would you place the aims of each institution you attended?

Subject teaching

Let's consider how these various types of education aims might look in the classroom. We can do this by focusing on subject teaching, taking as our example – as explained in Chapter 1 – the teaching of architecture.

If you look again at the above list of aims concerning individual development, you will no doubt be able to see various ways in which these might be applied in teaching architecture. For example, pupils might be taught about planning laws and processes, so they would be equipped to participate through local democracy in debates on developing the built environment. As regards social aims, pupils might learn about the most symbolic national landmarks or, say, their country's vernacular style.

13

From a conservative point of view, one might teach pupils about the architectural heritage – the canon of great architects such as Christopher Wren and Edward Lutyens, for example – or about laws and projects designed to ensure preservation of ancient buildings. From a radical point of view, pupils might be taught how to critique building developments – sub-standard public housing schemes, for example – and to propose change. The Commonwealth War Graves Commission (www.cwgc.org/education) has produced some excellent resources, for example, on how to prevent damage to memorials. They include a case study showing how the redesign of a memorial in Tower Hamlets, London, reduced the incidence of vandalism.

Pick a subject that you are involved with. Try to find examples of the following types of educational aims:

1. An aim concerned primarily with the individual pupil.
2. An aim concerned primarily with society (or the community).
3. An aim concerned with change.
4. A 'conservative' aim.

Bringing it all together

We have established two scales of education aim: the individual/social continuum and the conservative/radical continuum. We can place these two scales together to form a matrix:

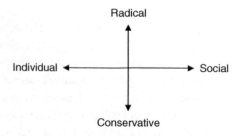

Figure 2.3 Matrix of aims

On this matrix we can place four combinations of aims. In the top-left quadrant we have radical-individualist aims – that is, aims concerned with the individual and designed to promote change. In the bottom left, we have conservative-individual aims – that is, aims concerned with the individual that value continuity. In the top right come radical-social aims – that is, aims designed to promote social change – and in the bottom right we have conservative-social aims (designed to promote continuity in society).

Consider your own educational aims.

1. Which quadrant(s) in the above model (Figure 2.3) do they fall into? You may find they fall into more than one; if so, which quadrant characterizes your aims best?
2. Suppose you planned to shift your aims towards one of the other quadrants: how could you achieve this? What changes would you make to your teaching?

Finally, we should note that there is a distinction to be made between explicit and hidden aims. The explicit aims are those that we articulate in public. The hidden ones are those that, without publicizing them or perhaps even articulating them, we actually follow.

Explicit aims are often to be found in official documents – school policies and prospectuses, departmental syllabuses, and so on. The problem is that these documents often provide no more than spin: they say what people think they *ought* to say – rather than describe actual practice. (A school might, for example, say that it values all pupils equally – but does it *really*?) This renders them useless as working documents. It is important, for you as a teacher to be clear about what your aims *really* are.

One of those aims – though you'll never see it said in any official document – is survival. We all want to get by, to keep the show on the road, to get to the end of the week. On its own that would not be a sufficient aim, but it is, surely, a perfectly reasonable one.

15

Though I'm reluctant to reduce the content of this chapter to a single sentence, if I had to, it would be:

Clarify what, ultimately, you are seeking to achieve in your teaching.

Further reading

Curriculum and Aims by Decker F. Walker and Jonas F. Soltis provides philosophical background for thinking about educational aims, especially in the chapter entitled 'The Aims of Education'.

The Aims of Education, edited by Roger Marples, is a collection of sixteen essays by philosophers of education. Essays that deal most closely with issues raised above include:

- 'Education without aims?' by Paul Standish.
- 'Critical thinking as an aim of education' by William Hare.
- 'The place of national identity in the aims of education' by Penny Enslin.

A short book on quality management is John West-Burnham, *Managing Quality in Schools: A TQM Approach*.

3

Needs

The previous chapter was designed to show the role of educational aims in a teacher's preparation. Once the question of aims has been considered, it is tempting to sit down and begin planning a course. But it's not that simple. As well as considering our aims, we need to consider the needs of the people involved in the educational process. This consideration provides the second cornerstone in the process of planning and preparing to teach.

A word should be said about the concept of 'need'. In educational discourse, the word is used rather loosely. Strictly speaking, a 'need' is something one cannot do without. It is rather difficult to say what needs (in this sense) there are in education. Casually, for example, we might say that we 'need' a supply of paper for our lessons – but there are plenty of examples of schools around the world that don't have a supply of paper, just as there are schools without roofs or walls or desks. They still function.

Discussion of 'needs' in the strict sense would rapidly take us into a speculative debate about the nature of human beings. Fortunately, we don't need to make things that complicated. Usually when we talk about 'needs' in education, we don't *really* mean 'needs' at all. For example, when we say a pupil 'needs', say, reassurance or more confidence or more time or more practice or extra support, what we usually mean is that the pupil would certainly *benefit* from such a thing and may even have a *claim* on it (a pupil may be deserving of extra support, for example). And if there's something that our pupils would benefit from or have a claim on, then we should consider it in our planning, whether or not this amounts to a need in the strict sense.

Whose needs?

When, a quarter of a century ago, I received my initial teacher training, the dominant image on the course was that of a teacher alone in a classroom with a group of pupils. That was a simplification even then. When I got into the classroom I sometimes found other people there (a school librarian, for example, or an advisory teacher). In addition, there were people who, though not physically present, certainly had a say in what was going on: the headteacher, for example, and, for some year groups at least, the examination boards. But although it was a simplification, it wasn't a gross one. For much of the time it did feel like just me and a group of pupils – rather a lot of them!

Today it isn't like that. The classroom has become, both literally and metaphorically, more crowded. Now there are much more likely to be other adults in the classroom with the teacher – teaching assistants especially. School inspectors visit more frequently. Outside the classroom itself, more people require more regular contact with the teacher. They include colleagues in school, especially line managers and co-ordinators and also other professionals – welfare officers, social services, health workers, police and so on. Parents' expectations regarding communication and consultation have tended to grow. Boards of governors and national governments have become more hands-on. The question 'Whose needs do I need to satisfy?' has become more complex.

There are two ways to react to this. One can certainly feel put upon. Lots of people want things from you and they all have views on what you should be doing, some of which pull you in contradictory directions. On the other hand, there are now a lot of people who care about what you are doing and can offer support and advice. The key point to grasp is that, like it or not, teaching as a collaborative venture is now a fact of life – and since that is so, it is important to make the most of it.

It is helpful here to draw on the concept of stakeholding. The term 'stakeholder' has been popular in management literature since the 1990s. Its popularity stems from the fact that it can be used to supplement or even replace the concept of shareholder. 'Stakeholder' is used to indicate that, in a business, many groups besides the shareholders – that is, the owners – may have something at stake. Stakeholders might include the managers, employees, suppliers, clients, local community and government. Stakeholder management is concerned with questions of how organizations do – or should – attempt to manage their various stakeholders and their interests.

Precisely because it is not solely concerned with ownership, stakeholder management has become a popular concern of management in the public and not-for-profit sectors as well as in the private sector. It is not surprising, therefore, that the concept of 'stakeholding' has gradually become more common in the world of education. Much of the discussion concerning stakeholding has been rather remote from the daily business of teaching classes. It has tended to focus instead on questions of governance. However, at a time when teaching has become, one way or another, more of a collaborative business, classroom teachers are very much in the business of managing stakeholders – even if they do not use the actual term.

Ask yourself who your stakeholders are. Who has something at stake resting on your teaching?

There are different ways of categorizing your stakeholders. Here is a reasonably broad taxonomy.

- The pupils.
- You, the teacher.
- The pupils' families.
- Other people in the school, including other teachers, ancillary staff, staff with management roles and school governors.

- Other professions involved with your pupils, for example, welfare and social workers, health professionals, the police.
- Those who will work with the pupils in the future, for example, in primary schools, middle and/or secondary schools, further and higher education institutions, and employers.
- Other parts of the educational world. For example, exam boards, professional associations (such as the General Teaching Council).
- The community.
- The state.

Learning about stakeholders' needs

Once you have identified your stakeholders, you can begin to consider their needs. Try working down your list and noting down what you already know about each stakeholder's needs. You will probably find this produces very mixed results. Some stakeholders – the government, for example, and the school management team – are likely already to have been very voluble over what they want from you. Other stakeholders – perhaps those who will work with your pupils in future, after they have left your school – you might know little or nothing about.

Where you have identified holes in your knowledge, you can begin to make good by taking educated guesses about each stakeholder. It is all too easy, however, to confuse one's presumptions with what stakeholders really want. When, for example, parents have been surveyed on what they want from their children's schools, the results often show a gap not only between parents' values and teachers' values, but also between parents' values and teachers' perceptions of parents' values.

It's important, therefore, to investigate stakeholder needs directly. This cannot, of course, be done all at once. It should be thought of as a gradual, long-term, process. A certain amount of information may be gleaned from reading printed or online documents. Train yourself to skim through publications such as the *TES* (not just the jobs pages!) and trade union bulletins (rather than simply discarding them or letting them pile up unopened).

Create a folder in your internet favourites list for education sites – you can include, for example, professional bodies such as the General Teaching Council and media links such as broadsheet newspapers that include education pages.

The most useful way to add to your knowledge of stakeholder needs is probably conversation. Try asking stakeholders what their concerns are, what they value about your school or college, and what they want out of it. One of the most useful pieces of in-service training I ever received was when my wife, who isn't a teacher, happened to observe some of my appointments at a parents' evening. She pointed out that I tended to talk *at* parents: they sometimes asked me questions, but I tended not to ask them anything. From that moment on, I changed the way I conducted parental appointments. I started to ask the parents questions to find out what they wanted to discuss. As a result, parents' evenings became both more enjoyable and more productive. The parents found out more about what they wanted to know – as opposed to what I assumed they wanted to know – and I received more help in return.

School life provides many opportunities for engaging with stakeholders – it's just that we don't always make the most of them. For example, if you visit an employer to discuss the progress of a pupil on a work experience placement, it is easy to focus exclusively on the question of how the pupil is performing. In fact, however, such visits can also yield information about employer perceptions and attitudes. Often it's just a case of keeping one's eyes and ears open and remembering to ask the right questions. Similarly, it's very easy when talking to representatives of the parent teacher association to focus on particular tasks – the latest fund-raising event, for example – rather than taking the trouble to find out what other aspects of school life concern them.

As well as making use of opportunities that arise naturally, it can be useful to deliberately find ways to engage with stakeholders. That is, it can be useful to network. Attending twilight courses or local open days, for example, can help to develop your understanding of stakeholders you meet there. Networking does takes time, but it yields many benefits. In general, it helps to make the business of teaching less insular, to spark ideas and challenge assumptions, and to broaden one's vision and one's horizons.

Look again at the list of stakeholders above. For each stakeholder, consider how you can use the following to gain information about their needs:

1. Printed or electronic resources.
2. Routine school activities.
3. Additional networking opportunities.

What other methods might also be useful?

Baseline assessment as part of needs analysis

To be able to respond to the needs of your pupils, it is helpful to conduct a baseline assessment. The phrase 'baseline assessment' is sometimes used by bureaucrats to refer specifically to assessment of pupils in their first half term of primary schooling. I use it here to refer to the assessment of pupils when you begin to teach them, regardless of the stage of education they have reached. Conducting a baseline assessment has many benefits. It can indicate what your pupils can or can't do; it can help to identify special needs; and it can indeed provide a marker from which you can assess pupils' subsequent progress.

Baseline assessment has gained an uncertain reputation in the profession because teachers sometimes rely on methods that may be very narrow and even inaccurate. Sometimes 'baseline assessment' is reduced to scoring pupils on a test or series of tests conducted in a particular session. When that happens, the results are often nonsensical. Let me give one example. Once, when I attended a parents' evening, a teacher told me that she had given my 4-year-old son 'zero for his baseline assessment'. On inquiry I learnt that this meant that when the teacher had taken my son out of the classroom to ask him lots of questions and complete a number of exercises, he had completely refused to co-operate. His response to her questions was simply not to say anything. I told the teacher I didn't particularly blame him, since he might reasonably have concluded that the whole process seemed to be designed for her benefit rather than his – and that in any case the 'result' would surely work in her favour, since the next time he was assessed the 'result', if he so much as opened his mouth, could be used to indicate that he'd made positive progress under her tutelage!

The point of this anecdote rests on the fact that the teacher seemed to think it was all very significant. What had actually happened is that the educational bureaucracy had defined 'base-line assessment' as one particular process, to be conducted in a single session, and that the process had on this occasion yielded a meaningless result. The teacher was under the illusion that she had conducted a baseline assessment, whereas in fact all she had done was follow through a bureaucratic procedure that, in this case, had *failed* to produce a baseline assessment. When I explained that I wasn't much more interested in this 'baseline assessment' than my son had been and that what I wanted to know was how he was getting on in class, the teacher was able to tell me a good deal about his work. She had observed him in class, listened to him read, looked at his handwriting and so on. She had, in other words, made a reasonably broad baseline assessment. The problem was that she didn't regard any of this data as 'baseline assessment'. Evidently all that had gone into his records was a series of zeros!

The above anecdote concerns just one incident. If, however, we treat it as a cautionary tale, we can learn from it a number of general points about baseline assessment. Baseline assessment works best when it:

- employs a number of methods, both formal and informal;
- is conducted over a number of occasions;
- combines quantitative and qualitative data;
- is interpreted, rather than taken at face value.

In carrying out your own baseline assessments, cast your net widely. Accumulate as much recent or current information as you can from existing sources. Sources might include portfolios of pupils' work, test scores, statements of special needs and pupil records.

You can supplement this information by your own observations and assessments when you begin teaching the class. It can be useful to set a wide-ranging series of tasks (designed to test a range of skills or areas of knowledge), without much preparatory teaching, early on in your time with the class.

Remember, above all, that assessment data needs always to be interpreted. This is easily forgotten. Numerical test scores, in particular, can look very objective and self-evident. But such scores only reflect pupils' performance on particular occasions as assessed against particular mark schemes. It cannot even be assumed that such mark schemes have been accurately applied, especially when a piece has not been double-marked.

As an example of the need for interpretation, let me give an example from my own experience. In my first year of teaching I was required to administer to an entry-year class what the local authority termed 'standardized tests'. They included a 'quantitative reasoning' paper, which included various types of mathematical questions. Some of the questions were arithmetical exercises that included brackets. Many of the pupils had not previously encountered the use of brackets in sums. The designers of the test had attempted to counter this by including in the test paper a few paragraphs of explanation. The idea that this would somehow standardize the tests, by placing pupils on an equal footing with pupils who had been taught brackets at their previous schools was ludicrous: the pupils in my class were in effect being tested on their ability to assimilate new information, from the printed word, instantaneously. Yet this test yielded a 'standardized' score out of a hundred which was duly recorded in pupil records. I can only hope that these results were never used as measures of the pupils' mathematical ability.

Bringing it all together

Needs analysis is one of those areas in which educators may learn from the literature of training, which often devotes extensive treatment to the topic. In *A Practical Guide to Needs Assessment*, Kavita Gupta summarizes common areas of needs assessment. Areas requiring analysis include the following:

- The subject to be taught.
- The learners.
- The learners' knowledge and skills compared to the knowledge and skills required.
- The learners' attitudes (e.g. towards learning and towards change).
- Problem-solving.

Pupil attitudes are clearly important, yet we often fail to give them explicit attention. There is a danger here of relying entirely on implicit methods, such as observation of body language, and of marginalizing the comments and attitudes that underlie them. Such reliance can make attitudes difficult to ascertain, accommodate or challenge. It can sometimes be useful instead to consult pupils directly, for example through a written survey on such matters as attitudes to the subject, self-perception of needs and pupils' own objectives. It is often best to structure such a survey in the form of a ranking exercise, so that the pupil is required to discriminate between items on a survey and so cannot give a blanket response. For example, rather than ask 'do you like . . .' or 'how much do you like . . .', it can be more revealing to ask pupils to 'put the following in order of preference'. The example that follows is based on a handout I have used with classes in secondary school and in adult education.

Studying Architecture: Your Objectives

(A) Different people want to get different things out of the subjects they study. Below are a number of possible objectives students might have for their Architecture course:

- I want the course to help me go on to study Architecture at a higher level.
- I want to get as high an exam grade from the course as I possibly can.

- I just want to enjoy the course and learn interesting things.
- I want the course to help develop my general skills.
- I want the course to help me move into a career in Architecture (or a similar area).
- I want to pass the course without being too worried about what grade I achieve.

In class we will discuss these objectives. After the discussion, please place these objectives in the order they apply to you. Put a '1' next to your top objective, a '2' next to your next objective and so on down to '6' for the objective that least applies to you.

(B) Please write below any other objectives you have for the course.

Though I'm reluctant to reduce the content of this chapter to a single sentence, if I had to, it would be:

Ask yourself who are the stakeholders in your classroom and what do they need?

Further reading

The chapter entitled 'Situation analysis/training needs analysis' in Peter Taylor's *How to Design a Training Course* provides a straightforward introduction to using stakeholder analysis when designing a course. He shows how it is useful to consider stakeholders' interests according to both their importance and their degree of influence.

In Chapter 2 of *The Psychology of Teaching and Learning* (pp. 18–25) Manuel Martinez-Pons outlines formal and informal methods for assessing the needs of stakeholders. There is a wide-ranging discussion in a chapter entitled 'Assessing learners' needs' by Janet Hobley in Fred Fawbert (ed.), *Teaching in Post-compulsory Education*, 2nd ed.

The best general text on stakeholder management is Andrew Friedman and Sarah Miles, *Stakeholders*. The treatment is comprehensive, lucid and well organized.

Jean Rudduck has written extensively about involving pupils in school development – see, in particular, *Improving Learning through Consulting Pupils*, co-authored with Donald McIntyre. For a focus on engaging with parents, see Garry Hornby, *Improving Parental Involvement*.

4

Context

During my pre-service training I did my teaching practice at a large co-educational school in the centre of a newly built, fast-growing, city. It was a community school on a campus, built next to a shopping arcade, that included facilities such as a swimming pool and theatre. The school was self-consciously Progressive. The headteacher was known to all – students, staff and parents – as Mike.

After I had qualified I began teaching in another large co-educational school. This was a rural school, tucked away on the edge of a small market town but in the centre of a vast, rural, catchment area. The school was a comprehensive that had previously been a secondary modern. *Nobody* addressed the head-teacher by her first name: she addressed the staff by their titles (Mr, Mrs, Miss, etc.) and demanded the same courtesy in return.

From there I moved to another rural school, this time situated in a village. This was predominantly a boys' school, although it had recently changed its admissions policy and admitted girls (well, a few) from the age of sixteen. It too was a comprehensive, though before that it was a grammar school. The school had no catchment area: that is no pupils were allocated to the school as a default option – each pupil's parents had to actively opt to send the pupil there.

And so on. The schools I have taught in have varied widely in terms of their size, location, intake, history and ethos. One lesson

I learnt very quickly was that context does matter. You can't simply take the same lesson and teach it in different kinds of schools – or, rather, if you do, the lesson will not remain the same: the process, the experience and the outcomes will alter according to the context.

This is a point that professional education and training, and the literature that supports it, often does not give sufficient attention to. In practice, the answers to all the 'how' questions – how you would design a lesson, how you would go about teaching a particular topic, how you would manage the class, how you would assess the students and so on – are always in part that 'it depends on the context.'

The difficulty here is that we lack a well-articulated model for discussing how context affects the educational process. In the standard texts on teaching, contextual variables tend to be reduced to a range of general factors – principally socioeconomic class, ethnicity, pupil age and sex. Each of these variables is undoubtedly important. For example, the community school mentioned above was markedly more working class than the former grammar school: that teaching in the two schools felt different was partly the result of this fact. The 'Further reading' section at the end of this chapter highlights a number of resources focusing on the implications of these variables.

The point of this chapter is not to add to the guidance that exists concerning these general factors. Rather it is to indicate the difficulties that arise from thinking only in terms of these factors. First, other, more local or specialized factors can get overlooked. The significance of the history of the school, for example, is often neglected in teacher training literature. Second, how general factors *combine* in any particular school can prove important. It's difficult to generalize about teaching on the basis of any one factor – what it is like to teach in, say, a single sex school or a rural school or whatever will depend in each case on which other variables are operative. The mix matters.

Consider any two or (preferably) three educational institutions with which you are familiar, drawn from the same phase of education.

1. Make a list of the ways in which they differ from each other.
2. For each variable on your list, consider how significant it is likely to be to the question of how to teach.
3. Overall, how might your approach to teaching vary between the institutions?

Aspects of context

We may summarize the above discussion by saying that

− context is dynamic: it is formed by the interplay of factors over time;
− context is always to some extent local.

For this to be useful, however, we need some more down-to-earth, detailed, categories with which to think. Here the literature of English language teaching (ELT) can be useful: ELT is taught in a very wide variety of contexts and so the professional literature tends to be more explicit about the subject.

In *Designing Language Courses*, for example, Kathleen Graves discusses 'what is meant by context' by developing a parallel between teaching and architectural design:

Imagine . . . you have been commissioned to design a house. Where do you start? Having watched [architects] design and oversee the building of houses . . . I know that if have to design a house you don't begin with sketches, because you have no basis for the design. You begin with specifications. For example, where is the site, how big is it, what are its particular features? What is the time line? What materials are available locally? And so on.

Graves concludes that 'designing a course is similar to designing a house. You need to have a lot of information in order to design a structure that will fit the context'. She provides a model of educational context under five headings, namely:

- The people (students and other stakeholders).
- The physical setting.
- The nature of the course and institution.
- Teaching resources.
- Time.

We have already considered some aspects of these contextual factors (Chapter 3, for example, discusses the role of stakeholders, including pupils) and others will be discussed elsewhere below. Here we will focus on (a) time and (b) physical setting.

Graves helpfully breaks 'time' into a series of factors, each of which can be considered in relation to planning. They are: (a) the overall time allocation of the course (the number of hours and the span of time), (b) the frequency of lessons, (c) the duration of lessons, (d) the timing of lessons (On which days? At what time of day?), (e) where lessons fit into students' schedules and (f) students' punctuality. To these I would add two more factors, namely (g) what interruptions to the course may be anticipated (for example, exam leave, field trips) and (h) how much time outside lessons may students be expected to devote to work for the course.

Using the categories identified above, critically examine your timetable and schedule for the term and/or year. In what ways does the consideration of temporal factors affect your planning and preparation?

Similarly, Graves breaks 'physical setting' into a number of different aspects. They are: (a) the location of the school, (b) the classroom – its size, the furniture it contains, the lighting, and noise and (c) the question of whether the teaching is always in the same classroom.

To see how such factors affect teaching, let's consider two of the schools that I have taught in. In one I taught in a ground floor classroom constructed of modern building materials. It was carpeted, clean and bright. Along one side of the room was a series of built-in drawers with a strong wooden top a couple of feet or so from the ground. At the front of the class was a walk-in, lockable, stock cupboard. Just outside the classroom was a small foyer, with enough room for a desk or two and a few chairs, around which was clustered three other classrooms. On the other side of the room was a fire exit, leading outside.

In the other, my classroom was on the second floor of an older, inter-war, building. The building was in a style known as 'post-office Georgian'. The classroom was again well lit, though the bottoms of the windows were higher off the ground, making the windows difficult to look out of. The tables were larger and heavier than those in the first classroom: they were sturdier, but more difficult to move. There was no carpet. The classroom was deeper than the first. At the back of the room was a lockable door providing the only entrance into a small stockroom that was also well lit. Outside the classroom was a brick corridor that ran the entire length of the building, with a series of other classrooms leading off along one side and a set of fire doors half way along.

Both rooms were, in their own ways, typical classrooms. Across the country, there must be thousands of rooms of similar styles. Yet though typical, they were obviously very different from each other – and the differences affected the kinds of lessons I planned.

The first room leant itself to flexible teaching: it was easy to pull back the furniture and for pupils to sit, entirely safely, on top of the drawers along the side of the room, thus creating space for drama work of various kinds. The carpeting helped to ensure that such work – and the moving of furniture – was not too noisy. And there were spaces (the foyer outside and, at a pinch, the stock cupboard) where one or two pupils could work away from the rest of the class.

The second room had the virtue of being larger, but it was much less flexible. I cleared a space in the stockroom where two pupils could work comfortably. That helped a little. But the only space outside was the corridor and that was quite unsuitable: noise echoed along it and so pupils in the corridor were likely to distract other classes. Lessons were inevitably more constrained.

In contrasting these rooms, I have focused on the practical aspect of the two spaces. This does not, however, entirely capture the difference. There is also the overall 'feel' of the space to be considered. The first felt convenient, comfortable, unremarkable but unobjectionable and not entirely unhomely. The second felt austerely institutional – the high windows, echoing corridors, the sheer rigidity all betokened a dull, drab view of schooling that needed actively to be countered.

Consider two educational spaces that are familiar to you.

- What values do the architecture and design seem to incorporate?
- How would you describe the feel of each space?
- What constraints would each space impose on your teaching there?
- And what opportunities does each offer?

Ethos

Above we have considered some of the contextual factors itemized by Kathleen Graves. As we've seen, Graves includes in her list of factors the nature of the institution. Here I would like to draw attention to one aspect of that factor, namely ethos. It is difficult to say exactly what ethos is. The *Oxford English Dictionary (OED)* characterizes ethos as 'characteristic spirit, prevalent tone of sentiment of a . . . community; the "genius" of an institution or system'. That seems to me to capture it pretty well, yet it does so only by using other words, such as 'spirit' and 'tone', which are also difficult to define. They are difficult not only to define, but also to measure. How would one construct, for example, an index of 'tone'?

Given these difficulties of definition and measurement, it is not surprising that the concept of ethos is rather under-represented in the professional literature. Look through the indexes of standard texts on teaching and you will often find the term 'ethos' missing. Similarly it is rather under-researched. Yet this does not at all mean that the ethos of an institution is unimportant.

Quite the reverse. Indeed, if you look and listen to the messages that schools and colleges send – for example to new staff or to prospective parents – you will see that a concern to communicate an ethos is high priority. When newcomers transgress the defining lines of an institution's ethos, they tend to be quickly alerted to the fact. There is usually a ready concern to communicate 'the way we do things here'.

So ethos matters, yet is difficult to pin down. How then to think about the role of the institution's ethos in one's teaching? There are two useful ways to get a hold of this concept. The first is to ask newcomers – new pupils, new teachers, teaching students, visitors and so on. Until they have got used to the ethos of the place, they will be conscious of the features that distinguish it and able to articulate those features. If there is a way of capturing this – for example, in informal notes or journal-keeping, or through conversation – this can prove invaluable. But this needs to be done very quickly, because most newcomers rapidly begin to adapt to the ethos of their surroundings and to take its distinguishing features for granted. I reckon that there is usually a window of a fortnight at most in which to capture a newcomer's observations before they lose their freshness of vision.

The second way to reflect on the ethos of your institution is to focus on one crucial aspect of it, namely the way that people around you see the relationship between teacher and pupil. When I think about the differences in ethos between the institutions I have taught in, they have always been reflected in (perhaps 'embodied in' would be more accurate) the way in which this central relationship is conceived. I am tempted to suggest that, where two institutions actually share the same view of the teacher–pupil relationship, any differences in ethos between the two places are likely to prove unimportant.

People's conceptions of the teacher–pupil relationship have two main components. The first is distance. Do the people around you think that the relationship should be quite close – characterized by, for example, friendliness, informality, personality, warmth and so on – or should it be more distant, characterized by formality, impersonality and coolness? It can be helpful to compare institutions by, however impressionistically, placing them on a spectrum according to the predominant views of the ideal distance between teachers and pupils as shown in Figure 4.1:

Close   ⟵   ⟶   Distant

Figure 4.1 Teacher–pupil relationship (distance)

The second component is status. What is the predominant view of the ideal relative status of pupils and teacher? Should they be on a level? Or should one party have a higher status than the other? And if so, how much higher? Again it can be useful to plot this on a spectrum (the higher the ideal status of teachers is supposed to be, relative to pupils, the higher on the spectrum as shown in Figure 4.2):

Relatively high status of teachers

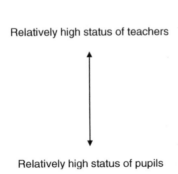

Relatively high status of pupils

Figure 4.2 Teacher–pupil relationship (status)

One can then combine these two to plot the overall position of the ideal relationship according to the predominant view in the institution as shown in Figure 4.3:

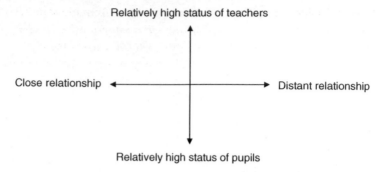

Figure 4.3 Teacher–pupil relationship (two dimensions)

(A) Consider educational institutions with which you are familiar. Try plotting them according to the predominant views of the ideal relationship between teachers and pupils. Note that it is the people's views of the ideal that we are concerned with – and it is the predominant view, not your own view, that we are concerned with here.

(B) What implications might the differences have for your teaching?

I suggest that, though the concept of ethos is a subtle one, it is useful on a pragmatic level to simplify the way one thinks about it. The working assumptions I have proposed here are:

1. Differences in ethos may be captured by focusing on differences in how the relationship between teachers and pupils is conceived
2. That relationship may be defined by two key variables – distance and status

Official documents published by educational institutions obviously need to be interpreted warily. They rarely say, for example, that 'we treat staff and pupils like dirt and tolerate low standards'! Yet, for the purposes of distinguishing ethos, it can at least be useful to look at differences in what institutions say they aim to do.

In the appendix to this chapter are statements from the websites of three educational institutions. The first is Stantonbury Campus (www.stantonbury.org.uk), a co-educational comprehensive school in Milton Keynes. The second is Dulwich College (www.dulwich. org.uk), an independent school for boys in suburban London. The third is Hampshire College (www.hampshire.edu), a post-compulsory liberal arts college in New Hampshire, USA.

Questions

Consider first the two schools, Stantonbury Campus and Dulwich College, as contexts for education. So far as can be ascertained from these documents:

(A) What do they have in common?
(B) What contrasts can you discern?
(C) Consider a course that you teach. What differences might you encounter in terms of how you might be expected to teach the course in each of these schools? To what extent might you conform to these expectations?

Now consider Hampshire College. I do not know whether any students from either of the two schools have actually gone on to Hampshire College, but supposing that they did:

(D) In the case of students from (a) Stantonbury Campus and (b) Dulwich College, what continuities and changes would they be likely to experience?

Bringing it all together

The argument of this chapter has been that, in planning and preparing to teach, context matters. The same lesson, delivered in different contexts, will have different outcomes (indeed, will in some sense turn out not to have been in fact the 'same' lesson). Context is a wide-ranging concept, one that is difficult to characterize. It certainly involves an interplay of factors over time. Those factors include: people; place; the nature of the course and the institution – including its ethos, resources and time.

I have left until last perhaps the most important consideration when it comes to deciding how context affects, or should affect, one's teaching. That is, there are always two questions involved:

1. What is the context in which one is teaching?
2. How does one respond to that?

It is undoubtedly useful to get clear what the context is – the more contextual information you can acquire, the better. But there is then a second set of decisions to make. To what extent should one seek to perpetuate the context as it is – to accept, support or promote it? And to what extent to challenge, modify or reform it?

Though I'm reluctant to reduce the content of this chapter to a single sentence, if I had to, it would be:

> Reflect on what you know about where you are teaching and ask yourself what the implications are for your teaching.

Further reading

Andrew Pollard, *Reflective Teaching* gives rather more attention to the question of context than do most textbooks on teaching. It includes a chapter entitled 'Social Context'. Justin Dillon and Meg Maguire, *Becoming a Teacher* includes a chapter on 'Excellence in Cities' (though not one on excellence in rural areas).

Kathleen Graves' thinking on context in relation to language teaching is given in *Designing Language Courses*.

Trentham Books publishes a number of books about education in relation to social context, focusing on the education of particular groups of pupils. These include: Marie Parker Jenkins, *Children of Islam*; Kamala Nehaul, *The Schooling of Children of Caribbean Heritage*; Farzana Shain, *The Schooling and Identity of Asian Girls*; Robert Jackson & Eleanor Nesbitt, *Hindu Children in Britain*; Mohamed H.

Kahin, *Educating Somali Children in Britain*; Ken Marks, *Traveller Education*; Jill Rutter, *Supporting Refugee Children in 21st Century Britain*; and Pat Thomson, *Schooling the Rustbelt Kids*.

Appendix: Documents from three institutions' websites

1) Stantonbury Campus

The Campus: Stantonbury Campus is a large and successful comprehensive school providing education for 2,750 students, including approximately 500 post-16. We aim to include all young people in our community and to help everyone learn from the different strengths individuals bring to the Campus.

The Campus combines superb facilities and opportunities for students with a small school friendliness and care based on five halls of approximately 500 students each. Four of the halls are for students aged 11 to 16, while the fifth caters for our post-16 students. Each has its own Head of Hall, team of tutors and specialist teaching and associate staff. Students are taught in their halls, while specialist facilities are shared with one other hall. Wherever possible, tutors stay with the same group of thirty students for the first five years of their education at the Campus.

Student Education and Development: We believe that young people learn and develop best when they and their families are treated with genuine respect and equal value. We therefore do all we can to break down artificial barriers between the adults who work here, students and their families. There is no uniform, everyone is known by their first name and we share facilities. This leads to warm relationships between adults and students. It also means our students are used to being listened to and having their point of view respected.

As our purpose statement makes clear, we are committed to learning in its widest sense. We believe all students can be successful learners and we work with determined optimism to help each individual achieve personal success. We want learning to be challenging and exciting for all our students. Knowing that learning happens in and out of classrooms, we provide a rich and varied extra curricular programme. Exchanges with France, Spain, Germany, Tanzania and India offer wonderful opportunities to students and staff.

Source: www.stantonbury.org.uk (visited 4 August 2008).

2) Dulwich College

We are academically selective and our boys are generally in the top 15–20 percent of the national academic range. They come from a wide range of backgrounds and have diverse interests which enrich the life of the College. Nearly all progress to degree courses at British universities.

Our principal aims are to provide:

- an appropriate academic challenge which enables each pupil to realize his potential;
- an environment which promotes a good work ethos and encourages all boys to acquire an independent and critical approach to learning;
- a wide range of sporting, musical and dramatic opportunities and co-curricular activities through which boys can develop a breadth of interests and learn to work co-operatively;
- a caring, supportive and well-ordered community which encourages spiritual and personal development where boys from a variety of cultural and social backgrounds can feel secure and equally valued.

The College benefits from historic buildings in a delightful environment; it has a distinguished tradition of inspired teaching and genuine scholarship. We seek to build on this to achieve our aim and so help current and future generations of Alleynians [i.e. former pupils] to be well prepared for life.

Source: www.dulwich.org.uk (visited 4 August 2008).

3) Hampshire College

Hampshire College was founded on the belief that the best education is the one a student builds around personal goals. Hampshire opened in 1970, created when presidents of four distinguished New England colleges sought a home for bold, influential – even radical – ideas in higher education. The result: a Hampshire education, shaped around a student's own interests, rather than the usual liberal arts formula. Advancing through three levels, or Divisions, students explore freely and widely across Hampshire's five interdisciplinary Schools.

To graduate, every student, with faculty advice and guidance, devises an individual program in which he or she attempts to ask – and answer – a question perhaps never posed before.

Beyond Hampshire's own substantial academic resources, students draw on those of Amherst, Mount Holyoke and Amherst Colleges and the University of Massachusetts, which together form the Five College consortium. Arguably, no other college in America offers students so much freedom – or so much support.

Source: www.hampshire.edu (visited 4 August 2008).

5

Cognition

This chapter and the three that precede it are based on the view that there are four cornerstones that you can use to support your planning and preparation. So far we have examined three of these – aims, needs and contexts. This chapter examines the fourth, namely cognition – its nature and the way that it is structured.

Most introductions to teaching consider learning. Typically, they consider how pupils learn and what implications this has for teaching. This is right and proper, except that often they miss out a stage. As well as asking how pupils learn, we need to consider *what* it is they learn – and this requires us to consider what cognition is.

The question of what cognition is has a long history in philosophy, especially in the area of epistemology, and psychology. It is, therefore, difficult to develop an informed overview. Yet as teachers we do need some model of cognition, otherwise we do not know what it is we teach.

This chapter, therefore, takes a pragmatic view of cognition. It seeks to provide a working model. The model is, on the one hand, intended to be sufficiently simple to be readily understandable, memorable and communicable. And, on the other, sufficiently multi-faceted to help teachers plan ambitiously.

The model divides cognition into four components:

1. Declarative knowledge: including both empirical and conceptual knowledge.

2. Procedural knowledge: including skills, techniques and methods.
3. Outlooks: including attitudes, dispositions and orientations.
4. Events: including judgements and decisions.

This chapter outlines, with examples, each of these components and considers how they may be applied when planning to teach.

Declarative knowledge

The first component is probably what most of us think of when we think of knowledge. It consists of facts, data, information and so on. Often when we begin a sentence by saying, 'I know that . . .', we are referring to this kind of knowledge. It includes the kind of knowledge that features in quizzes – who won the FA Cup in a certain year, who succeeded Elizabeth I and so on. Such knowledge may be trivial or it may be of practical or cultural importance – knowing which materials conduct electricity, for example, or who painted the Mona Lisa. It may be hard-earned (say, the times-table for 13, which I have yet to learn) or taken-for-granted (I no longer have to think which pedal is the clutch).

To illustrate each component of our model, we can draw examples from football. The following are examples of this first component. I know that:

- each team starts with eleven players on the field;
- only goalkeepers may handle the ball;
- Pele scored 1,000 goals in his career;
- the World Cup finals occur every four years.

It can be helpful to sub-divide this component in two ways. First, we can make a broad distinction between empirical and conceptual knowledge. Roughly speaking, empirical knowledge is in principle observable. For example: water consists of hydrogen and oxygen; sea water is salty; the tides are influenced by the gravitational pull of the moon. My empirical knowledge of football includes the facts that Wayne Rooney plays for Manchester United (at least, at the time of writing) and Celtic FC once won the European Cup.

Conceptual knowledge entails knowledge of ideas. For example, I know that the circumference of a circle is equal to the diameter times [π], even if I have never seen a perfect circle or tried to measure one. In football, I know the 10-yard rule (opposing players must stand at least ten yards from the ball before a freekick is taken), even if I am not always good at judging whether players are in fact observing it.

A second useful sub-division is that between extensive and intensive knowledge. This is the distinction we have in mind when we talk of the difference between knowing a little about a lot or a lot about a little. When we say we know a little about a lot, we are referring to our extensive knowledge. Extensive knowledge is superficial. In contrast, intensive knowledge goes below the surface. Intensive knowledge is deep.

For example, my knowledge of geometry is more extensive than intensive. It isn't in fact very extensive, but I can at least name several components of geometry – acute angles, parallel lines, equilateral triangles, and so on. I can, however, remember very little about their properties or the relations between them. I therefore have almost no intensive knowledge of geometry.

Similarly, I have, as a casual follower of football, developed a reasonably extensive knowledge of the game. I wouldn't win any quizzes, but at a push I could probably name all of the English football league teams. But about many of these teams I know very little. It would not, for example, take very long to write out all I know about, say, Port Vale FC. There are some areas of football I have more intensive knowledge of – Cambridge City FC, for example, who I watch quite often – but these areas are very narrow. Overall, one could say that my knowledge of football is neither very extensive nor very intensive, but tends more to the former than the latter.

Overall, then, we can summarize the first part of our model with a matrix.

Table 5.1 Declarative knowledge matrix

Declarative knowledge	Intensive	Extensive
Empirical		
Conceptual		

Consider a subject that is not your main specialism. Explore your declarative knowledge of it in the light of the concepts above (Table 5.1). Ask yourself, in particular:

(A) What kinds of empirical knowledge do you have? List some of the data.

(B) What kinds of conceptual knowledge do you have? List some of the concepts you understand.

(C) In which areas of the subject is your knowledge most extensive? How extensive would you say your knowledge of the subject is overall?

(D) In which areas of the subject is your knowledge most intensive?

Procedural knowledge

The second component of our model is procedural. In education, we seek to develop pupils who not only possess plenty of empirical and conceptual knowledge, but also know *how* to do many things. We want them to be able to say not only 'I know that . . .' or 'I know of . . .' but also 'I know how to . . .' or 'I can . . .'

This kind of knowledge includes skills, techniques and methods. When referring to this component, educators often make do with just the term 'skills'. To use 'skills' as a shorthand for procedural knowledge may be satisfactory, provided one remembers that it *is* shorthand. The danger, however, is that using 'skills' exclusively leads us to neglect other forms of procedural knowledge. We may either forget that (besides skills) techniques and methods form part of education – or we may just assume that they are all the same.

The *OED* defines the terms as follows:

- Skill: 'Capability of accomplishing something with precision or certainty; practical knowledge in combination with ability; cleverness, expertness'.
- Technique: 'Manner of artistic execution or performance in relation to formal or practical details . . . the mechanical or formal part of an art, also skill or ability in this department of one's art . . .'
- Method: 'A special form of procedure adopted in any form of mental activity, whether for the purpose of teaching and exposition, or for that of investigation and inquiry' and 'In a wider sense: A way of doing anything, especially according to a defined and regular plan; a mode of procedure in any activity, business, etc'.

The above definition of 'technique' seems to me too narrow, unless we broaden the definition of 'art', for example, to include craft, sport and technical activities.

I hope that by now the problem with reducing all procedural knowledge to 'skill' is becoming clear. It is true that the notions of skill, technique and method overlap: they all represent ways of getting things done; the above definition of 'technique' utilizes the word 'skill'; and the looser definitions, in particular, of method (e.g. 'a mode of procedure') seem to make room for the notion of skill.

Yet in other ways these concepts differ from each other. The more tightly defined a 'method' is, the more it may emerge as distinct from, even opposite to, skill. People often define and systemize methods precisely to exclude the need for skill. In statistics, for example, rigorous sampling methods are developed precisely so that individual researchers can employ them without needing to acquire a skill.

In fact, teachers sometimes invent methods precisely to compensate for a lack of skill on the part of their pupils. When I was at school, many of my teachers would tell me to check my work, without actually specifying how to do so. To me, then, checking seemed very much a skill – and not one I had a good grasp of. Then the person who taught me German gave the class a method for checking (e.g. first ensure that adjectives agree with nouns in terms of number; then check they agree in terms of gender etc.) Suddenly, checking seemed something that required little skill beyond recalling one's basic knowledge of German: instead, the method provided something you plodded through, step-by-step – something that you followed.

Again, by way of illustration, let's consider some examples from football. There are some examples of procedural knowledge in football that fit the above definition of 'skill' very well. One example is learning to trap the ball by slightly withdrawing one's foot as the ball approaches. Some examples, however, seem to fit the definition of 'technique' better. An example might be learning which part of the ball to strike in order to make it swerve in a certain direction. And then there are examples of procedural knowledge that seem better described as 'method': learning to play in a four-person defence, for example, and to advance up the field in line with each other.

'Method', therefore, can turn out to be very different from 'skill'. 'Technique' often turns out to be a halfway house – something perhaps less defined, less algorithmical, than a method and, like a skill, requiring more practice. The educational point here is that as teachers we need to be alert to the types of procedural knowledge that we teach. To the extent that skills, techniques and methods are different things, they need to be taught differently. It was, after all, only when one of my teachers conceived checking as a method rather than a skill that I learnt how to do it.

Consider a field in which you have extensive 'know how'. This might be a school subject or it might be some other area of knowledge – a hobby or a sport, for example. Try to distinguish (a) the skills, (b) the techniques and (c) the methods that you have learnt.

Outlooks

Attitudes, orientations and dispositions all entail matters of outlook or perspective. The *OED* defines 'attitude' in terms of 'settled behaviour, as indicating opinion' and a 'settled mode of thinking'. Disposition it defines in terms of 'bent, temperament, natural tendency; inclination', while to orient(ate) is to 'determine how one stands'. They thus differ from each other, though not as much as they differ from other components of our model, such as skills.

What attitudes, orientations and dispositions have in common is that they are all relatively stable. They all last for periods of time: they may be temporary, but not momentary. Attitudes are perhaps least stable, most quickly and easily changed. They each tend to be bound up, at least to a degree, with personality. Orientation is perhaps more deliberate, more a matter of decision, than disposition.

Whereas teachers have no reluctance over teaching procedural knowledge, such as skills, they are often wary about the idea of teaching attitudes, dispositions or orientations. This is in part because it is difficult to do: precisely because they tend to be 'settled', and often run deep, they can be difficult to change. In part the wariness is also because education concerned with attitudes and so on can sound worryingly like indoctrination. (However there is a logical distinction: from the fact that all indoctrination is concerned with attitude, it does not follow that all education concerned with attitude is indoctrination.)

In fact, however, as educators we cannot afford to ignore this component of our model. For one thing, as perhaps their definitions suggest, the attitudes, dispositions and orientations of our pupils tend to act as filtering systems. They help to determine what those pupils attend to, focus on, or value. Outlooks can therefore be extremely powerful. When they are constructive, they can make the acquisition of declarative and procedural knowledge efficient. (For example, a concern for quality tends to be a powerful driver of success in education.) But when they are not receptive, they can render even good teaching of such knowledge ineffective.

Moreover, the learning of new outlooks can itself form a valuable part of education. Scientists, for example, need to learn to develop scepticism, to question hypotheses, to demand and assess evidence. Sociologists need to learn to study, in some sense dispassionately, the way that people's opinions (religious belief,

for example) are formed and the influence their opinions have –
regardless of whether the sociologist shares those opinions. And
so on.

Once again, let's look at some examples from football. Coaches
are well aware that performance depends on outlook. They talk,
for example, of developing competitiveness, confidence, self-
belief, hunger for success and so on. The importance of these
factors among fans is equally clear – consider, for example, the
way that home crowds' perceptions of incidents in the game
so often differ from those of referees.

Consider your own characteristic (a) attitudes, (b) dispositions and
(c) orientations either in or towards your specialist subject. (Try,
so far as possible to distinguish between the three types.) Ask
yourself:

(a) Which are the most important?
(b) How did they develop? What would you say they are based on?
    How, if at all, have they changed?

Mental events

It is common to believe that, if we just teach pupils enough – if
we ensure they develop their declarative and procedural knowledge, and perhaps their attitudes, dispositions and orientations –
they will know how to arrive at judgements and how to make
decisions. But, as many people who have refereed a sports
match for the first time can confirm, this is not necessarily the
case. One can be very well informed and well intentioned, and
yet still make poor judgements or give bad decisions. Similarly,
players can work hard in training, develop their skills, go into
a match in the right frame of mind – and yet proceed to make
poor choices.

Judgements and decisions always require application of
knowledge – and application is not always straightforward.
Often it requires practice and experience – as anyone learning

to drive will confirm. Judgements and decisions are always in some sense pragmatic. They are events. They need to be made here and now, often on the basis of incomplete and uncertain information. We need in our planning, therefore, to give attention to the question of how we are going to help pupils exercise judgement and make sound decisions.

Subject teaching

Let's consider how these ideas can be applied in subject teaching. As usual, we will use the example of architecture.

In one town near where I live, there is a debate over the future of the market square. At present it is used two days a week for a traditional market. The rest of the time it is used as a car park. The market traders are obviously happy with this and many of the residents support the market. Some people, however, argue that it is a waste of a prime site. They argue that the site should be developed to provide an extension to the modern shopping centre that is adjacent.

Suppose this issue provided the focus for a module in an architecture course. The model of cognition that we have developed in this chapter can be used to help create a rounded, cognitively balanced, module. Here are some examples:

Declarative knowledge: Several types of empirical knowledge are useful here. Examples include facts about: the site (e.g. its dimensions); the authorities concerned and the decision-making processes involved; and the laws and regulations that might apply. Similarly, several types of conceptual knowledge would prove useful. Examples of relevant concepts include: revenue; taxation; heritage; consultation; tendering; vested interest; scarcity; competition; and so on. A mixture of extensive and intensive knowledge is likely to be required. For example, pupils might look briefly at a number of other towns in order to collect a range of possibilities and then in more detail at one or two comparable sites to see how the way they are used works in practice.

Procedural knowledge: Relevant procedures here are likely, between them, to cover the spectrum of skills, techniques and methods. They might range from surveying the site through surveying opinion to forecasting footfall and drafting aesthetic designs.

Outlooks: There would be opportunities both to investigate stakeholders' viewpoints – how, for example, do traders, shoppers, developers and councillors look at these things? There would also be the opportunity to employ a range of perspectives – economic, aesthetic, legal and so on.

Mental events: The project in fact lends itself ideally to the development of judgement and decision-making, for example through simulated meetings. Pupils could be asked to evaluate a range of proposals, using a varied set of criteria, and to make a recommendation.

Bringing it all together

Thanks to the influence both of Progressive thinkers and of management thinking, educators have long been concerned to move on from the view that education is simply about learning facts. In many ways this is healthy – except that in looking for a contrast to facts, there has been an over-reliance on the term 'skill'. The term has been used increasingly lazily and mindlessly: it has tended not only to drive out the other procedural terms, such as technique and method, but also the terms we've used above to describe outlooks and mental events – attitudes, dispositions, orientations, judgements and decisions. One hears educators talk, ludicrously, of such things as patience or ambition or enterprise as a skill. The danger is that we then either attempt to teach as skills things that aren't – or that we simply omit those things that aren't skills and so imbalance our pupils' cognitive development.

This chapter has been based on the assumption that we need to understand what it is we're trying to teach – what cognition is – so that we can be sure we teach it adequately. In particular, it has sought to provide a balanced, workable, model that can be used in planning and preparation. The following chart summarizes the model:

Table 5.2 Cognitive components

Component	Sub-components
Declarative knowledge	Empirical/conceptual Extensive/intensive
Procedural knowledge	Skills Techniques Methods
Outlooks	Attitudes Dispositions Orientations
Mental events	Judgements Decisions

The next chapter uses this model as a building block in curriculum design.

Reflect on either a course you teach or a course you have studied. Focus on one part of it – say, a module, unit or sequence of lessons lasting about a month. Analyze it using the chart above (Table 5.2). So far as possible, list a few examples of each sub-component.

Though I'm reluctant to reduce the content of this chapter to a single sentence, if I had to, it would be:

When planning to teach, don't allow the notion of 'skill' to swamp other kinds of cognition: give explicit attention and due weight to all the main cognitive components.

Further reading

I have found books on sports coaching and psychology much more helpful than texts on teaching. Sports professionals have often thought long and hard about such aspects as skill acquisition and attitude formation. It can be stimulating, therefore, to consider parallels between, on the one hand, coaching and training and, on the other, teaching and learning in skill acquisition. Useful, accessible, sport texts include Kevin Wesson, *Sport and PE*.

6

Curriculum

In the past I have sometimes seen documents, purporting to be curriculum documents, that did little more than list the subject matter that pupils were expected to cover over a certain period of time. They were set out in list form and read like tables of contents. Thankfully, it is a long while since I have seen such documents. Most educators today are aware that there is more to a curriculum than this. But what else, precisely, is required beyond the listing of subject matter?

In *The Cubic Curriculum*, Ted Wragg recommends that we should see curricula as at least three-dimensional. The first dimension consists of school subjects. These can be set out as a one-dimensional list. For example:

- Biology.
- Geography.
- Modern language.
- Physical education.
- Technology.

and so on.

On the second dimension Wragg lists cross-curricular themes. These concern issues that people believe should figure in a curriculum, but not simply as separate subjects. These might include, say, environmental education, which might be taught across a number of subjects such as geography, biology, techno-logy and so on. Similarly, creativity might be taught across a number of subjects – perhaps even all of them.

By combining these two dimensions, we can construct a matrix. For an example, see Table 6.1:

Table 6.1   Curriculum matrix

	Environment	Creativity	Health
Biology			
Geography			
Modern language			
Physical education			
Technology			

This is certainly an improvement. But Wragg suggests we should go further by adding a third dimension consisting of modes of teaching and learning. Examples include imitating, observing, discovering and so on.

We can now envisage the curriculum as a cube: on one axis we set out the various subjects; on the second come the cross-curricular themes; and, on the third, modes of teaching and learning.

Although Wragg gives examples of what might feature on each axis, he is less concerned to push any particular version of the curriculum than simply to establish a multi-dimensional view of the curriculum. This chapter will, therefore, adopt a three-dimensional view while using rather different categories from Wragg's. I have chosen to use different categories here, in part to simplify the model and in part to make it more appropriate for individual teacher's planning (Wragg's book was aimed more generally, at the level of whole school and policy development).

The first dimension: subjects

In Wragg's model, the categories on this dimension consist of whole subjects. Wragg notes, however, that these categories can of course be sub-divided. For example, physical education may be sub-divided into topics such as gymnastics, dance and team games. This is obviously more relevant for individual teachers.

By way of illustration, let us consider, as in previous chapters, the example of architecture. We could imagine such a course being divided into categories such as the following:

- Building materials.
- Structural principles.
- Functions.
- Styles.
- Laws and regulations.

Each of these may be further sub-divided. For example, see Table 6.2:

Table 6.2 Subject matter

Building materials	Brick
	Concrete
	Wood
	Glass
	Stone

For the moment, however, we will stick at the level of main categories within each school subject. We will be more concerned with sub-categories in the next chapter.

For your own subject, list the main sub-divisions. For example, you may use the headings of monthly or half-termly units, so that you have a list of say half a dozen or a dozen categories for a year's course.

The second dimension: cognitive components

On the second dimension, Wragg places cross-curricular themes. Here we will replace these with cognitive components. This is not to imply that cross-curricular themes are unimportant. It is simply that in this chapter we are concentrating on the most basic building blocks and aiming to keep the resulting structure as simple as possible. We will consider cross-curricular themes in the next chapter.

The cognitive components are those that we established in the previous chapter, namely:

- Declarative knowledge.
- Procedural knowledge.
- Outlooks.
- Mental events.

As we have seen, each of these may also be sub-divided. Again, however, we will keep things simple at this stage by dealing only with the four main categories above.

Let's put into these categories some examples from our architecture course. Take the example of architectural styles. We may wish pupils to learn certain key concepts (e.g. texture, volume), important styles (e.g. baroque, modernist) and the names of associated architects (e.g. Wren, Le Corbusier). We may also wish them to learn how to do certain things – estimate square footage, for example, or write a critical essay. In addition, we may wish to teach pupils to adopt certain kinds of outlook – appreciating heritage, for example, or looking for ways to improve buildings. And, finally, we may wish them to make judgements and decisions, for example by deciding which building is the most impressive of its type or which would most deserve a subsidy for renovation.

We can now begin to map out the curriculum using a two-dimensional matrix. Table 6.3 shows a fragment from our architecture curriculum:

Table 6.3 Curriculum construction (two dimensions)

Module	Declarative knowledge	Procedural knowledge	Outlooks	Mental events
Style	Major styles, e.g. baroque, classical, Gothic, modernist Major names, e.g. Wren, Soane, Pugin, Le Corbusier	How to write a critical review	Aesthetic	Ranking buildings according to a set of criteria

The third dimension: modes of learning

On the third dimension of his curriculum model, Wragg placed modes of teaching and learning. He proposed categories such as telling, imitating, working in a team, observing, discovering and practising. Here I should note a point of disagreement. I question the point of including modes of *teaching*: surely it is learning that is paramount. What matters in a curriculum is how pupils learn, rather than how they are taught – which is not, of course, to say that questions over the types of learning do not have implications for teaching too.

Be that as it may, the model developed in this chapter resembles Wragg's, at least by including modes of learning. However, I have defined these differently. Instead of the kind of categories used by Wragg (as listed above), I'll use just four categories. These are:

– Theoretical learning.
– Concrete learning.
– Reflective learning.
– Active learning.

The advantage of concentrating on these four categories is that it makes our model simple and powerful.

The categories correspond to those developed by David Kolb in his theory of experiential learning. What I have called 'theoretical learning' corresponds to what Kolb terms 'abstract conceptualization'. According to Kolb, an orientation on the part of the learner towards this type of learning emphasizes the use of 'logic, ideas, and concepts' and 'a concern with building general theories'. Learners of this type enjoy 'systematic planning' and 'manipulation of abstract symbols'. Kolb says that they value 'the aesthetic quality of a neat conceptual system'.

In contrast to theoretical learning is what I have called 'concrete learning'. According to Kolb, an orientation of learners towards 'concrete experience' emphasizes 'being involved in experiences'. It places the stress on 'a concern with the uniqueness and complexity of present reality as opposed to theories and generalizations'. Learners of this type tend to be 'intuitive decision makers' and to 'function well in unstructured situations'.

Reflective learning (in Kolb's terms, learning from 'reflective observation') emphasizes 'understanding the meaning of ideas and situations by carefully observing and impartially describing them'. According to Kolb, learners with this orientation 'enjoy intuiting the meaning of situations and ideas' and 'looking at things from different perspectives'. They form opinions from their own thoughts and feelings.

In contrast to reflective learning comes active learning (in Kolb's terms, learning from 'active experimentation'). Learning of this type emphasizes 'practical applications', 'a pragmatic concern with what works' and 'doing as opposed to observing'. Learners of this type enjoy 'getting things accomplished' and are prepared to take risks to achieve their objectives.

There is a danger with such taxonomies. The risk is that learners will label themselves according to the taxonomy and then adopt behaviour that re-enforces the stereotype. For example, a learner might decide that she is, say, a 'concrete learner' and then seek only opportunities for concrete learning. She might then turn her back on, say, opportunities for theoretical learning ('No, I'm a concrete learner!'). Such behaviour would more or less guarantee that the learner fails to develop her capacity to learn in other ways.

Such self-restricting behaviour is not, however, advocated by Kolb himself. Rather, the implication of his work is that courses should be sure to incorporate all these types of learning, so that learners encounter material presented in a number of ways. Indeed, Kolb has become famous for the 'Kolb learning cycle', which incorporates all four types of learning outlined above. (In writing this book, I have tried in each chapter to cater for the four modes of learning.)

Let's briefly consider how we could incorporate these modes of learning into a course on architecture. Theoretical learning could be introduced through teaching theories from physics and engineering – in the area of mechanics, for example. Concrete learning could be introduced through field trips to particular places and to the use of detailed case studies. Pupils could draw on reflective learning by being encouraged to examine their own experience of buildings in the past, while active learning could be incorporated through a requirement for pupils to create their own designs.

Consider a unit or module in a course you teach or a course you have studied and identify examples of opportunities for:

- Theoretical learning.
- Concrete learning.
- Reflective learning.
- Active learning.

If you cannot find examples for a certain category, consider how the lack could be remedied.

The three dimensions: the curriculum as a cube

Our model is now complete. We have established the three dimensions. In the first dimension we have categories drawn from the subject matter of the curriculum. In the second dimension, we have cognitive categories (declarative knowledge; procedural knowledge; outlooks; mental events). And on the third dimension, we have modes of learning (theoretical; concrete; reflective; active).

The model can then be used to map and plan the curriculum. Wragg suggests establishing a standard terminology in order to facilitate discussion of the cubic curriculum. He suggests that each category that cuts across other dimensions should be called a 'channel'. Thus we would have, for example, a 'mental events' channel and a 'reflective learning' channel. Each intersection of channels from each dimension could be termed a 'cell'. Thus the part of the architecture curriculum that combines, say, learning about building materials (a first dimension channel), declarative knowledge (second dimension) and 'concrete learning' (third dimension) would form a cell (an example of such a cell would be learning about the properties of brick, with some examples of different types of brick in evidence). A group of cells considered together could, adds Wragg, be referred to as a 'block'. Nothing, however, hangs on this terminology: it is proposed for convenience only.

Familiarize yourself with the terminology by considering a part of a course that you teach or have studied. Identify a few examples of:

- Channels.
- Cells.
- Blocks.

Now let's consider how this model may be used in planning a course. I suggest that you begin by considering the first dimension, that is, subject matter. Consider one channel at a time (e.g. in the architecture course that we have been developing, we might start with a module on building materials). List the types of work that you might cover in this module.

Now consider another dimension – let's say the third dimension, that is, modes of learning. Ask yourself whether each channel is adequately filled. (That is, does the course include sufficient opportunities for theoretical, concrete, reflective and active learning?) If you feel any of these channels is not adequately filled, design a learning opportunity to make good the lack (e.g. if you feel there is insufficient opportunity for active learning, create an exercise, experiment or project for pupils to do).

Now consider the remaining dimension – here, the cognitive components. Again, ask yourself whether each channel is adequately filled. (Does the course do enough to incorporate mental events – that is, judgements and decisions – for example?) Again, decide how to remedy any lack.

Gradually we can plan an entire course this way – drafting initial plans for each module, assessing them in the light of the model and redrafting where necessary. By, in effect, examining the course cell by cell, we can ensure that the plan is rigorously tested.

The course does not need to include every conceivable cell. That is, it is not necessary for each and every second and third dimension channel to be filled for each subject module or unit. But patterns of absence are likely to be significant. If, for example, you find your plans include few opportunities for concrete learning – perhaps because you are not a concrete learner yourself – then the likelihood is that you need to revise your plans in order to avoid disadvantaging pupils who learn best in this way. Similarly, if you find that, say, the plan for an entire term involves little in the way of judgements and decisions on the part of pupils, you need to consider whether you are really promoting a balanced, rounded, programme of cognitive development.

> Consider a course that you teach or have studied. Focus on one first dimension channel (i.e. one topic or area of subject matter). Examine it in relation to (a) each second dimension channel (i.e. each cognitive component) and (b) each third dimension channel (i.e. each mode of learning). How adequate would you say the course is or was? Where would you consider it to be lacking? How could this be remedied?

Bringing it all together

One sometimes meets teachers who opt out of the responsibility of curriculum planning. They tell you, whether contentedly or complainingly, that it's all been done for them – by the government, or the examination board, or the school management team, or whoever. This is always an over-complacent view. In the first place, officially prescribed curricula are rarely presented as total curricula; typically they are couched rather in terms of what at all costs needs to be covered – the essential core. In the second place, such specifications rarely cover all three dimensions of the curriculum. They leave teachers, therefore, with both the scope and the responsibility to plan.

Moreover, it may well be that there are more dimensions to consider than the ones discussed in this chapter. In a chapter called 'Introducing the Cube' at the start of his book, *The Cubic Curriculum*, Ted Wragg says:

> Actually, it isn't a cube. It's a multi-dimensional hyperspace, but *The Multi-dimensional Hyperspace Curriculum* does not exactly have a ring to it. Like all models the cubic curriculum is a simplification of the real world, an attempt to reduce enormous complexity down to something one can try to get inside and explore.

If you had to add a fourth dimension to our model of the curriculum, what would it be?

Though I'm reluctant to reduce the content of this chapter to a single sentence, if I had to, it would be:

When planning a course, think three-dimensionally.

Further reading

Ted Wragg's model is outlined in *The Cubic Curriculum*. David Kolb's theories are explained in *Experiential Learning*.

7

Planning in the medium and short term

Consider a complete novice – say, someone on day 1 of a pre-service training course. Asked what a lesson plan should consist of, the novice might well say it should specify the subject matter to be covered in the lesson – and probably also the activities that pupils would be expected to do. And even complete novices fairly rapidly learn that a little more is needed. Say:

- A specification of the aim of the lesson – what it's designed to achieve.
- A list of the resources needed.
- A specification of how the pupils' work will be assessed.

This gives us a five-point plan:

1. Aim.
2. Content.
3. Methods.
4. Resources.
5. Assessment.

This type of plan will actually get us quite a long way. It is workable. But from a professional teacher we should certainly expect more.

Opinions differ about exactly what a teaching plan should consist of and how many elements there should be. However, just as *The Hitch-hiker's Guide to the Galaxy* revealed the answer to the riddle of the universe ('42'), so I can now reveal the definitive answer to how many elements a plan should contain. The answer is 20.

Before we examine the 20 elements, we need to consider the question of time scale. Professional practice requires plans covering three time scales. First, there is the long-term plan, that is, a curriculum, showing the structure of courses over an entire year (and so, collectively, over a sequence of years). Second, there is the medium-term plan, often referred to as a 'scheme of work'. This covers a sequence of lessons. There is no set time scale for this, though most such plans probably range from about a month to half a term. Third, there is the lesson plan.

Planning the curriculum has been dealt with in Chapter 6. This chapter will deal with the medium- and short-term plans. For these I have found that it is useful to use a common 20-point framework. This should, however, be applied differently to the two levels. With schemes of work, it is certainly helpful to include statements under all 20 headings. With lesson plans, it will prove useful at least to consider each of the 20 elements when formulating the plan, but the written plan that results may well omit some of the elements. There is an advantage to using the same conceptual framework for both types of plan, since this makes the relationship between scheme of work and the lesson plan very clear. This makes it easier both to derive lesson plans from the scheme of work and to check that the lesson plans, cumulatively, do indeed cover the scheme of work fully.

Enough by way of theory. Let's look at the framework itself.

The perfect plan

The perfect plan will include information on the following:

1. Aims.
2. Objectives.
3. Assessment data.

4. Scope and content.
5. Pedagogical methods.
6. Teacher's expectations.
7. Learning activities.
8. Homework.
9. Differentiation of learning.
10. Progression in learning.
11. Other curricular links.
12. Time.
13. Space.
14. Resources.
15. Language.
16. Ancillary staff.
17. Risks.
18. Assessment.
19. Evaluation method(s).
20. Review procedure(s).

The rest of this chapter will consider these elements one by one. With some elements the aim will be to provide fresh discussion: with others, it will be to refer the reader to the relevant passages elsewhere.

1. Aims

You may feel that we have dealt with the topic of aims in Chapter 2. The aims that we dealt with there, however, were large scale, overall aims – the type of aims that apply to the curriculum, whole courses, and one's overall approach to teaching. Aims such as 'enabling pupils to achieve formal qualifications' or 'equipping pupils with the ability to earn a livelihood' are, on their own, too broad for medium- and short-term planning. We need more fine-grained aims for those time scales, though they should certainly be shaped by our overall educational aims.

My advice for formulating medium- or short-term aims is to think about it – but not to think for too long. It is possible to be *too* clever at this point. The advantage of keeping aims simple is that it makes them easier to remember and easier to communicate to other people. For the same reason it is helpful not to have too many aims for each unit.

Often the main aim can be specified with reference to one particular cognitive component. This might concern subject matter, for example. For instance, in a course on architecture, we might say that the main aim of a module on building materials is for pupils to know the main properties of a number of materials and the main implications for architectural design. Or we might focus on some other cognitive component – for example, as discussed in the previous chapter, to learn how to write a critical essay (an example of procedural knowledge) or to develop an appreciation of a site's heritage (an example of outlook).

It is usually best if the main aim is stated in a single sentence or even a single clause. This makes for clear-headedness. It is easy when teaching to lose sight of the wood and see only the trees – it is useful, therefore, to be able to ask oneself, 'What am I trying to do here?' A crisply stated aim will then help you to see the wood again.

2. Objectives

Objectives are similar to aims in that they specify what you are trying to achieve in a lesson or sequence of lessons. They differ in that they are narrower and more specific. Thus if the aim for a sequence of lessons is for pupils to learn how to read maps, the objectives might include learning to interpret contour lines and to recognize standard map symbols.

Giving careful thought to the setting of objectives helps effective teaching in a number of ways. It helps you as the teacher to clarify what you are trying to achieve. It also helps you to communicate this to your pupils and other stakeholders.

Objectives should specify what pupils should be able to do as a result of their learning and at what level they are expected to perform. It is commonly said – rightly, I believe – that objectives should be SMART, that is,

- Specific.
- Measurable.

- Achievable.
- Relevant.
- Time-bound.

This formula is successful for a number of reasons. In the first place, it helps to ensure that what you are writing really are objectives (the requirement for them to be specific and time-bound helps to distinguish objectives from aims). It helps to make objectives motivating (the 'A' and the 'R' proving particularly helpful here). And it helps with subsequent assessment and evaluation (the 'M' and 'S' proving important here).

That objectives should ideally be measurable helps to determine the type of verbs you will use in their formulation. Try to avoid using words such as 'understand', 'appreciate', 'think'. Developing aspects of pupils' understanding or appreciation of, or thinking in, a subject may be fine as an aim, but these things are difficult to observe and hence to measure. Verbs specifying actions – such as 'calculate', 'construct', 'define', 'demonstrate', 'indicate', 'list', 'name', 'perform', 'record', 'select' or 'use' – are preferable for this reason.

Two common errors are to set too many objectives in total and to set too many that are same-y. One of the advantages of shaping one's plans around objectives is that they can help you to focus on what is essential. This effect is dissipated if you encumber yourself with a long list of objectives. To ensure variety of objective, try to include two contrasting types of objectives, namely:

- 'hunting' objectives;
- 'fishing' objectives.

The former occur where everyone knows what kind of response the teacher is after. The latter occur where it is less certain what sort of outcome is expected. Asking pupils to research particular dates in the history of architecture may involve the former; asking them to write a comparative study of two buildings may involve the latter.

Suppose three pupils were given the task of completing an investigative project on a famous architect. Using the guidance given above, suggest three possible objectives for the project.

3. Assessment data

This concept is discussed in the section on baseline assessment in Chapter 3. It should be added here that the principle of baseline assessment can be applied as a short-term principle as well as a long-term one. That is, as well as assessing what pupils know when they begin a new school year or phase of education, we can also check what they know at the beginning of a lesson or sequence. This may include checking what has been understood and remembered from the previous lesson.

4. Scope and content

It is obviously necessary to decide what the lesson or sequence will be about. With reference to the cubic model of the curriculum, outlined in the previous chapter, think particularly of the cells formed by the intersection of the subject channel (first dimension) and the declarative knowledge channel (second dimension). What is the subject of the lesson(s)? How much will be covered? Which concepts and data will it deal with?

5. Pedagogic methods

The plan should include a list of what the teacher is going to do. In particular, how are you going to present material and set tasks? This is crucially important to the teacher and also to any support staff in the lesson(s). It is of less interest to any other stakeholders reading the plan.

6. Teacher's expectations

This category provides a good example of why it is desirable to plan comprehensively. It is all too easy to go into a lesson without having thought through one's expectations. This I've learnt from a number of occasions. One goes into a lesson feeling fully prepared – you have defined the objectives, prepared the resources, rehearsed the content and so on – only to realize during the lesson that one is fuzzy about the level of expectation. Pupils respond to your tasks – they participate in discussion, write text or whatever: but are they performing at a level you expect?

It may emerge during a task that the pupils themselves are unsure of the level of expectation – in which case it is always harder to retrieve the situation than it would have been to make things clear at the beginning. Or you may find that the pupils themselves seem clear of the level of expectation, but you aren't: you feel hesitant about whether the responses are acceptable, whether they should be commented, challenged or whatever. Such uncertainty has a habit of communicating itself to the class pretty quickly. The more the uncertainty spreads, the more the presumed level of expectation falls to the lowest common denominator.

This applies to expectations concerning both quality of work and behaviour. One solution is to dramatize the lesson(s) in one's mind as much as possible before teaching. If you are setting some group work, for example, what sort of activity or discussion are you expecting to see or hear? Where is there a danger that pupils may get the wrong end of the stick? What can you do to prevent this misunderstanding or ambiguity arising?

Note that these questions are much easier to answer if the setting of objectives has been completed rigorously. Appropriate objectives usually imply some level of expectation.

It may be helpful to have in mind four notional levels of performance:

- Beginning.
- Emerging competence.
- Proficiency.
- Expertise.

Reflect on a few typical activities in a course that you teach. In each case, consider how the same activity would look under two very different sets of expectations. What could be done to make the level of expectation clear on each occasion?

7. Learning activities

What work will pupils be required to do? This question needs to be answered on two levels. The first refers to the mode of learning. In the cubic model of the curriculum developed in the previous chapter, we specified four (third dimension) channels, each based on a mode of learning, namely theoretical, concrete, reflective and active learning. The question here is which of these channels will the lesson(s) involve?

The second level is more detailed. It concerns questions such as which particular resources pupils will use, which part of the DVD they will watch, how many questions in an exercise they will attempt. The guidance given in Chapters 8 and 12 will prove useful here.

8. Homework

Homework can significantly extend pupils' learning and help to raise achievement. But it won't do so automatically. It needs to be set appropriately. The learning should be purposeful. In particular, it needs to be properly integrated into the curriculum, rather than merely an add-on. Ideally, tasks should be challenging but achievable. If they are self-motivating too, so much the better. The important point is to seek to make homework a quality learning experience, rather than a method of filling time for the sake of it.

Be wary of setting homeworks consisting of 'finishing off class work'. This can make life hard for slow learners – they end up with more than other pupils to do. The cumulative effect can be punishing. 'Finishing off' work can also encourage pupils to work superficially or carelessly, seeking to polish off as much work as possible in class in order to minimize homework.

Similarly it can encourage pupils to idle away class time on the basis that they can always 'finish it at home'.

Be wary too of basing homework too often on writing. Many pupils find unsupported writing tasks difficult or demotivating. And if pupils do respond by covering lots of paper, the marking load for the teacher may be unmanageable.

Look for opportunities to treat homework as 'prep', that is, preparation for the next lesson as opposed to a sequel to the previous one. Pupils may be asked to prepare for lessons by, for example, collecting resources, bringing ideas or suggestions or researching information. Contributions of this kind can help pupils to feel they have a stake in the lesson that follows.

Overall, bring to bear on your planning of homework the same approach and professionalism that you bring to bear on your lesson planning. In particular, use the same curriculum model (Chapter 6) and the approach to objectives explained above.

9. Differentiation of learning

Pupils differ from each other in all kinds of ways – personality, attainment, cultural background and so on. This means that, even if they all experience the 'same' lesson(s), they will experience it differently. Moreover, we may well decide not to provide the 'same' lesson(s) to all our pupils in any case. Instead, we may decide to provide different activities.

The control of these differences is known as 'differentiation'. The decisions that you make over the level and type of differentiation need to be included in your plan. The approach to differentiation is discussed in more detail in Chapter 12.

10. Progression in learning

Although we have discussed in Chapter 6 what the curriculum should consist of, we have said nothing so far concerning the order in which units should occur. What should come *when*? This entails questions of pupils' progression – how they move from one piece of learning to another. This too will be discussed in more detail in Chapter 12.

11. Other curricular links

We saw in Chapter 6 that Ted Wragg included 'curricular themes' in his cubic model of the curriculum (as his second dimension). Although I omitted these from the model of the curriculum developed in this book, I said that this was not because I thought they were unimportant. It is because links between parts of the curriculum are important that they need to be included in your plan.

Note that I have preferred the term 'links' to 'themes'. This is because 'themes' tends to encourages a focus on subject matter (though not necessarily in Wragg's own thinking). For example, if we talk about the environment as a cross-curricular theme, the tendency will be first to consider where environmental information and concepts (i.e. declarative knowledge) are taught in the curriculum and to look for links between such instances.

And of course there is nothing wrong with that. Quite the reverse. It is a good way of helping to re-enforce learning between different curriculum areas and to avoid unnecessary repetition. (I well remember the tedium as a pupil when I was required, for example, to draw diagrams of a blast furnace in three different subjects for three teachers who evidently never spoke to each other.) It also identifies opportunities for teachers from different subjects to come together to form cross-curricular projects, which can both prove refreshing and provide cohesion.

But the problem comes, however, if cross-curricular links are seen *only* in terms of information and concepts. Some of the most exciting opportunities occur in other channels relating to other kinds of cognitive component – what in Chapter 5 we have termed procedural knowledge (skills, techniques, methods), outlooks (attitudes, orientations, dispositions) and mental events (judgements and decisions).

In one school where I was teaching English I worked collaboratively with a teacher of Humanities. In one year group we taught the same group of pupils. We realized that we could both include work on Ireland in the course. We decided to teach this subject matter at the same time of year and to share plans so that we could each refer to each other's lessons. This we felt would help pupils to make connections.

I remember that we got very interested in this collaboration across the curriculum. Unfortunately, the pupils seemed to show no interest in the phenomenon at all. I don't think it did any harm, but at the end of the unit I couldn't really point to any evidence that we'd added anything to the pupils' learning.

We also discovered that in another, more advanced, year group, we were both doing some work on close reading. In my lessons, we were focusing on the close reading of literary texts. And in the History lessons the focus was on the close reading of primary source documents. Though there was no significant overlap in terms of subject matter, there was in other ways: in the language of our curriculum model, there were similarities in some of the skills, attitudes and dispositions we wished to develop, but also some differences – especially in orientation.

In this example, our efforts to co-ordinate our teaching did seem to bear some fruit. Though we had not set the experiment up as a rigorous research project – and so lacked hard evidence – the reflections of those involved did seem to indicate some benefits. Perhaps it is significant that the stimulus for collaboration came in part from comments by pupils ('this is like what we're doing in English, sir').

The point of these two anecdotes is not to suggest that curriculum links at the level of content never come to anything, nor that curriculum links at other levels always succeed. Rather it is simply to issue an invitation, which is to look for opportunities to extend the development of cross-curricular links beyond the level of information and concepts.

12. Time

In medium-term planning we are most concerned with time in terms of the number of lessons or weeks required by a scheme of work. In short-term planning we are concerned with the use of time within lessons. This is covered in detail in Chapter 9.

13. Space

In medium-term planning we are most concerned with space in terms of the rooms or facilities available. In short-term planning we are concerned with the use of space within lessons. This is covered in detail in Chapter 10.

14. Resources

Preparation of resources is discussed in detail in Chapter 8.

15. Language

The place of language development within lesson planning is discussed in Chapter 11.

16. Ancillary staff

Ancillary staff may feature in planning in four ways. First, as discussed in Chapter 3, one needs to consider their needs as stakeholders. Second, you may seek to involve them directly during the planning process itself. Third, ancillary staff should certainly feature within the plan. What should ancillary staff contribute? How should they be deployed? What will they be doing in lessons?

Fourth, ancillary staff should be among the beneficiaries of the plan. That is, you are writing the plan not only for your own benefit, but also for other stakeholders so they can see what you are doing. As we've noted already in discussion of some of the items above, a comprehensive plan helps you to communicate with ancillary staff and helps them to understand what you are trying to achieve.

17. Risks

Your plan should include an assessment of any risks to health and safety. Indeed, in many countries there is a statutory requirement for teachers to assess risks to their pupils. To use an English legal term, teachers have a 'duty of care'. It is important to identify hazards in advance and to decide who is likely to be at risk, what the level of hazard is, and what action needs to be taken in advance to ensure that no unacceptable risk is taken.

In addition, you need to consider other kinds of risk. What happens, for example, if a crucial facility is unavailable? Or if unscheduled interruptions or absences occur? This is akin to continuity planning in business. In teaching, as in the theatre, the show most go on.

Remaining elements: (18) Assessment, (19) Evaluation and (20) Review Procedure(s)

Questions of assessment, evaluation, and review are discussed in Chapter 13. Suffice it to say here that, although these activities are mostly performed towards the end of the teaching process, they should certainly – as explained above in the introduction to this book – feature in your plan. One needs to consider *beforehand* how pupils' work is going to be assessed, how you will evaluate the lesson(s), and what kind of procedures you will use to review your work with regard to future practice.

Bringing it all together

In the introduction to this chapter we discussed the possibility of a five-point plan (aims, content, methods, resources, assessment). We have covered much ground since then. The 20-point framework is considerably more professional and rigorous. If it feels at all over-engineered I would re-iterate that it need not be used as comprehensively for each and every lesson as it should for formulating schemes of work. I would emphasize, however, that care in planning will maximize your chances of success. And having a well constructed plan does wonders for one's confidence when entering the classroom.

In many places the elements of the plan were related to concepts that we developed in the discussion of the curriculum in Chapter 6. The intention here has been to encourage coherence between long-term, medium-term and short-term planning.

Below are samples of draft plans for (a) a scheme of work (Table 7.1) and (b) a lesson (Table 7.2).

Table 7.1 Sample scheme of work

Scheme of Work	Architecture of Christopher Wren
Aims	Ensure that pupils acquire a rounded, critical, knowledge, at an introductory level, of Wren's contribution to architecture.
Objectives	Pupils will be able to:
	1. Name (a) types of buildings designed by Wren and (b) an example of each type.
	2. Recognize a range of Wren's best known buildings.
	3. Either (a) indicate through diagrams typical aspects of Wren's style or (b) create, through drawing, an imaginary Wren-style building.
Assessment data	Grades on previous stage in the subject vary from Level 5 to Level 7, with one pupil (X) on Level 8. Spelling ages vary from 10 to adult.
	Four pupils appear on the special needs register:
	⁓ A and B are dyslexic.
	⁓ C has behavioural difficulties and has a learning support assistant for some of the lesson time.
	⁓ X is listed as gifted/talented.
	P and Q have Punjabi as their first language.
Scope and content	Context: timeline; Wren's life and times; other architects of period.
	Survey of Wren's buildings (extensive knowledge).
	Case studies (intensive): St Paul's Cathedral; Wren Library (Cambridge).
	Reception: what people have said about Wren's buildings; reactions to buildings; Wren's reputation.
	Architectural concepts, for example, baroque; facade [complete list in syllabus outline].
Pedagogical methods	Powerpoint presentation (introduction).
	Case studies (demonstration with slide show, followed by pair exercise).
	Manage library lesson(s): mini-research projects.
	Support individual and small group work (research).
	Chair group presentations on research and whole class discussion.
	Revision of study methods for (a) library and internet research, (b) planning and drafting and (c) presenting.
	Supervision of completion of individual assignments.

(Continued)

Table 7.1 Continued

Scheme of Work	Architecture of Christopher Wren
Teacher's expectations	Classroom display and project presentations sufficiently detailed and explicit to convey knowledge to a peer group who had not studied the unit. Mini-project to include at least three stages (plan, draft(s), final copy).
Learning activities	Construct classroom display. Completion of quiz. Pair work on structured case study materials. Library and internet research. Small group and whole class discussion (evaluation of critics' comments; compiling a guide to key features of Wren's work). Individual mini-project including drafting and presentation.
Homework	Background reading/internet research. Observation of buildings' facades, plus report. Preparation for main assessment task.
Differentiation of learning	X to work with partner on mini-project on the baroque. Ensure pupils A & B use structured materials for research and homework tasks and for mini-project planning. Ensure pupils A, B, P & Q provided with (a) glossary and (b) writing frames for report.
Progression in learning	Look back to initial research task at start of the course: lists of famous buildings and architects. Use similar method next term for study of Frank Lloyd Wright.
Other curricular links	History: Great fire of London. Design and technology: method of planning and working through drafts of designs.
Time	Two sessions per week for half a term.
Space	Classroom. Library. Also home(work), virtual space (internet).
Resources	Powerpoint. Slides. Atlases. Copies of maps of London. Music of the period. Display materials. Textbook (case studies). Library.

Table 7.1 Continued

Scheme of Work	Architecture of Christopher Wren
	List of recommended sources. Internet [detail URLs]. Handout: quotations from critics. Test paper. Self-assessment handouts. A3 paper, pens, drawing equipment. Support materials: research and writing frames; glossary.
Language	Specialist terminology, for example, facade [complete list in syllabus outline]. Listening: - teacher instruction nb Powerpoint presentation, case study slide shows, study skills revision; - within pairs and groups; - to group presentations; - period music. Speaking: - process work: pairs and groups; - products: group presentations. Reading: - library research (printed and online reference, non-fiction) nb skimming and scanning; - teacher resources nb handouts, slides; - each other's work in draft from and in presentations. Writing: - process: plans; notes; - drafting presentations; - product: finished presentations/display; - individual mini-project; - end of unit test.
Ancillary staff	Brief library assistant, consult over recommended sources, reserve key books. Brief learning assistant, provide copy of course materials and assignments, discuss how to support pupil C in pair and group work. Office staff to photocopy handouts before unit starts.
Risks	Technology failure nb slide show. Some homeworks difficult to assess. Need for care when observing buildings for homework. Need to confirm library bookings.

(Continued)

Table 7.1 Continued

Scheme of Work	Architecture of Christopher Wren
Assessment	Informal: group presentations of research findings. End of unit quiz-style test. Visual: mini-project (features of Wren's style; imaginary building). Oral presentation of mini-project.
Evaluation method(s)	Compare grades to previous end of unit project. Targets for numbers of pupils reaching: (a) emerging competence, (b) proficiency and (c) expertise. Measure accuracy of pupils' self-assessments.
Review procedure(s)	Discuss with learning assistant and library assistant within two weeks of completion. Compare pupil attainment between two main tasks. Note changes required to (a) presentations, (b) formulation of assignments for next time round. Note changes required for overall study method (in time for unit on Frank Lloyd Wright).

Examine the draft scheme of work above (Table 7.1) in the light of the cubic model of the curriculum (see Appendix A). What opportunities can you suggest for improving the scheme of work by applying concepts from the model?

Table 7.2 Sample lesson plan

Architecture of Christopher Wren: Key characteristics	
Aims	Contribute to achieving the aim of the scheme of work, that is, 'Ensure that pupils acquire a rounded, critical, knowledge, at an introductory level, of Wren's contribution to architecture'. In particular, establish a list of characteristics of Wren's work.
Objectives	1. Establish a long list, orally and in note form, of possible characteristics of Wren's work. 2. Finalize a short list of key features.
Assessment data	nb dyslexia (pupils A & B). Pupil X on gifted and talented register.

Table 7.2 Continued

Architecture of Christopher Wren: Key characteristics	
Scope and content	Architectural characteristics (introduce jargon where appropriate). Wren's style.
Pedagogical methods	Explain objectives of the lesson. Small groups report to rest of the class. Plenary: establish list of characteristics, using whiteboard.
Teacher's expectations	Each presentation to last 3–5 min. Pupils to keep a running list of characteristics in note form.
Learning activities	Giving and listening to presentations. Deciding (after listening and through whole group discussion) which characteristics to include in plenary list.
Homework	None applicable (n/a) in this lesson.
Differentiation of learning	Provide pupils A & B with outline frame for note-taking. Pupil C to collaborate with teacher on informal assessments of group presentations. Pupil X to draft own list of key characteristics and include jargon terms. Ensure pupils A, B, P & Q have glossary to hand.
Progression in learning	Re-enforce habits of successful oral presentations (itemized in previous unit) Plenary list to provide basis for pupils to prepare for final assignments.
Other curricular links	Frameworks for note-taking (see differentiation above) used in other subjects.
Time	Briefing: 10 min. Presentations: 35 min. Plenary: 15 min.
Space	Seats and desks in rows. Presentation from front.
Resources	Whiteboard. Groups' prepared work (electronic presentation, sugar paper).
Language	Listening: primarily to presentations. Speaking: formal presentations; whole-class plenary. Reading: from screen (presentations, plenary) and own notes. Writing: notes during presentations.

(Continued)

81

Table 7.2   Continued

Architecture of Christopher Wren: Key characteristics	
Ancillary staff	N/a in this lesson.
Risks	Movement between presentations – ensure bags and leads stowed.
	Timing: may not get through each group's complete presentations (have plan B).
Assessment	Informal assessment of group presentations (Work prepares for final assessment task).
Evaluation method(s)	Timing: how well did schedule work?
	Did lesson produce desired list of characteristics in the plenary?
Review procedure(s)	Focus on whether instructions for groups' (a) research and (b) presentations have proved clear and workable.

> Examine the draft lesson above (Table 7.2) in the light of the cubic model of the curriculum (see Appendix A). What opportunities can you suggest for improving the scheme of work by applying concepts from the model?

Though I'm reluctant to reduce the content of this chapter to a single sentence, if I had to, it would be:

Time spent planning is rarely wasted.

Further reading

Five short, practical books are Graham Butt, *Lesson Planning*, K. Paul Kasambira, *Lesson Planning and Class Management*, Donna Walker Tileston, *What Every Teacher Should Know about Instructional Planning*, Leila Walker, *The Essential Guide to Lesson Planning*, and my own *100 Ideas for Lesson Planning*.

Janice Skowron, *Powerful Lesson Planning* provides a weightier discussion, well illustrated with examples.

A concise, pragmatic guide, written in a training context, is Tom Goad, *The First-Time Trainer*. As with many resources for trainers, the discussion of objectives is particularly strong.

In 'Organizing teaching and learning: outcomes-based planning', Vaneeta-marie D'Andrea distinguishes between learning object-ives and learning outcomes. This excellent essay is to be found in Fry et al., *Handbook for Teaching & Learning in Higher Education*. Though the focus is on higher education, much of her discussion of concepts may be applied to other sectors too.

8

Resources

Throughout this book we have been developing the image of the work of planning and preparation in terms of a three storey building. The first, second and third storeys consist, respectively, of long-, medium- and short-term planning. To this image we may now add a set of windows, representing educational resources – the thinking being that resources enable pupils to look out at the world, whilst also helping to shed light.

This chapter, then, is concerned with the key questions concerning resources at the stage of planning and preparing to teach. Which resources, of what type, should we use? How should we select or create them? What should we plan to do with them?

Resources and their use

Let's switch metaphors for a moment and think of resources as levers. Just as one can gain mechanical advantage through leverage – it's easier to open a door by pushing at the side farther from the hinge, for example – so resources can make teaching more powerful. To gain the most leverage, however, we need to select resources well and to use them effectively. This requires careful planning and preparation.

Here we can make use of a simple model. Think of a triangle. At one point we have the teacher. Teachers here have a dual role: they are both resources in themselves and users of resources.

At the second point of the triangle we have ready-made resources. These include purpose-made resources – textbooks, educational software, gymnastic and laboratory equipment and so on. Ready-mades also include resources that have not been designed specifically for educational purposes, but which may be used as such. For example, in art teachers may use scraps of card or plastic, while in language teaching they may make use of packaging, such as wine labels, displaying examples of the target language. In this chapter we will concentrate on purpose-made resources.

At the third point of the triangle we have resources created by teachers. These may be of various kinds – worksheets, assignments posted on the school intranet, Powerpoint presentations and so on.

The model, therefore, looks like this:

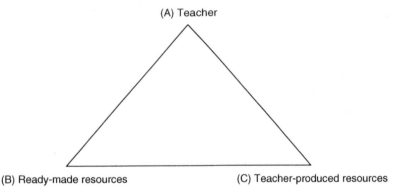

Figure 8.1 Resources in the classroom

The following is an A–Z of resources (just about, with a little help from search engines!) In your own work, what possible resources could you add to this list?

Audio recordings; books; computers; DVDs; e-books; files; a globe; handouts; the internet; jars; kvisu (the search engine at www.kvisu. com); the library; music; newspapers; *objets trouvés*; posters; quizzes; rulers; software; textiles; video; worksheets; examination papers; Yellow Pages; zuula (another search engine, www.zuula.com)

Let's briefly consider ready-made and teacher-made resources in general. Purpose-made educational resources, such as textbooks and educational software, offer certain advantages. Their production values (the use of colour, their construction, the finish of the materials and so on) are often high. They tend to have been professionally designed, edited and piloted. They are often tailored to particular courses.

But purpose-made resources have characteristic weaknesses too. If they are mass-produced, they're unlikely to suit to any specific context perfectly. After all, the producer is unlikely to have consulted you over your educational aims or conducted a needs analysis of your stakeholders. Moreover, the quality of resources varies and so the resources still need to be evaluated. They may be biased, perhaps for political or commercial reasons, or embody values that we don't wish to support – excluding or stereotyping minorities, for example. They may also require a heavy initial investment of cash, even when they offer good value over the long term.

In contrast, resources created by teachers may well be very well adapted to the context. That, typically, is their great strength: they are created for use by particular classes in specific settings. They also often cost little to produce. Often, however, there are also disadvantages. Precisely because they are bespoke, they may be difficult to transfer between context: what makes a resource suitable for one teacher or one class may make it less suitable for another. Moreover, resources can be very time-consuming to produce and difficult to preserve, store and retrieve. They also, frankly, can be poor in quality and even error-ridden. Examples of poor legibility, spelling mistakes, punctuation errors and shaky grammar are more likely to be found in teacher-made resources than in professionally produced ones.

The purpose of our triangular model, therefore, is not to suggest that one category of resources is better or worse than another. Each has its own advantages and disadvantages. The teacher has, as a result, always to make a critical judgement over which resources to use.

The purpose of the model is rather to display the choices available. The key point here is that it is not necessary to position a lesson at any of the points of the triangle. It's also possible to work between the points and within the triangle. That is where many of the most interesting opportunities in the classroom lie.

Let's look at some options. First, consider the space between you as the teacher (point A) and ready-made resources (B). What should be the relationship between you as teacher and the resources? In one instance, the resources may play a supportive role. You drive the lesson, drawing on resources for particular purposes – for example, you ask the pupils to turn to a certain page of an atlas in order to see a map of a country under discussion. If we were to locate such a lesson on the triangular diagram above (Figure 8.1), we would place it nearer to point (A) than (B).

In another instance, however, you might be replaced or supplanted by the resources. For example, pupils work directly from the resources, while you provide additional support only if they get stuck. On the triangular diagram, we would place this type of lesson much closer to point (B).

Work positioned near point (B) may be very productive – for example, when a teacher is absent, or when a pupil is working at home or where for purposes of differentiation some pupils are working independently. It can, however, be problematic. Teachers sometimes adopt a passive, uncritical role. Then the aims and values of the course come to be dictated by the resources. Provision is based not on a needs analysis, but on the resource producer's view of the needs of the market in general. In place of context-sensitive teaching we have lessons that, in effect, merely follow a script created by an absent producer. To avoid this, it is important when planning to make a deliberate, informed, decision about the relation between you and the resources in the lesson.

For a course with which you are familiar, try to envisage lessons located at various points along the line between (A) and (B).

Now let's consider the space between the teacher (A) and teacher-made resources (C). Here the relationship between teaching and resource will have been decided in advance and may even be built into the design of the resources. The closer the lesson lies to point (A) – the more teacher-driven, rather than resource-driven – the easier it will be to design the resources: you can explain each resource as you use it. Such resources may simply consist of material to be discussed or referred to – sets of data, for example. These resources will, however, be difficult to use independently, for example, when a pupil is trying to catch up after missing a lesson. They will also be less transferable between teachers.

Resources designed for more resource-driven learning – that is, in situations closer to point (C) – may be used more independently. They can, however, be more difficult to develop. Often such resources are best developed gradually – beginning as resources that need explanation and then, as you gain experience of how to explain them and of how pupils respond to them, edited into standalone resources. Indeed, many professionally produced resources begin as teacher-made resources that first go through this process of refinement.

If you have made some resources yourself, select a few of them to reflect on. Use the following questions as prompts:

1. Where on the line between (A) and (C) would you locate each one?
2. Which resources could be developed more for independent use?
3. Are there any resources that, with development, could be produced professionally?

Now consider the space between ready-made resources (B) and teacher-made resources (C). This space is perhaps the richest in opportunities. This is best articulated in the world of English language teaching (ELT), where many teachers find themselves provided with coursebooks ill-suited to the contexts in which they are teaching (which in ELT can be very varied indeed). A number of researchers and trainers in ELT have developed ways for teachers to use coursebooks without simply following them as a script. Much of their thinking is applicable in other subject areas.

Ian McGrath identifies four 'evaluative processes' available to teachers when adapting coursebooks (and by extension, I suggest, other types of resource). They are:

1. Selection (deciding which material to use and then using that material unchanged).
2. Rejection (omitting or cutting material).
3. Adding material.
4. Changing material more radically, for example, by replacing it with material from other sources.

McGrath divides the third of these categories, that is, addition, in two. There is *adaptation*, where you 'add' to the material by extending it or exploiting it more fully; and there is *supplementation*, where you introduce some fresh material to be used in addition to the original resource.

McGrath's taxonomy of processes offers a way of navigating through the space in our model between ready-made and teacher-made resources. Processes (3) and (4) (i.e. addition – especially in the form of supplementation – and radical change) provide opportunities for teaching in this space. And even the second process, rejection, may be thought of as a movement away from ready-made resources towards teacher-made resources: by editing out part of the ready-made resource, the teacher is in effect making it his or her own.

Consider a few ready-made educational resources with which you are familiar. What potential can you see for:

- Using them selectively, omitting some of the material?
- Adaptation: extending the material or using it more fully?
- Supplementation: bringing in fresh material to use in conjunction with the original resource?
- Radically changing the resource, for example, by replacing parts of it?

Readability

The first of the 'evaluative processes' above was 'selection'. One of the most important criteria for selecting resources is readability. It is useful, therefore to have a method to assess readability.

One option is to use quantitative measures. Numerous such measures have been developed, some of which are cited in the 'Further reading' section at the end of this chapter. Many involve counting syllables and words in a text in order to calculate the average number of (a) syllables per word, (b) words per sentence and (c) syllables per sentence. These scores are then converted through formulae into an index of readability. Typically the formulae work on the assumptions that (a) long words tend to be harder to read than short ones, (b) long sentences tend to be harder to read than short ones.

These assumptions chime with common sense. It is not surprising, therefore, if (at least when used to assess the *relative* readability of two or more texts), they often produce sensible results. But the assumptions aren't always accurate. For example, one may find with two sentences that are statistically similar (in terms of words and syllables) that one is really more readable than the other. Moreover, what we are usually concerned with is comprehension, since if our pupils can in some sense read a text but are unable to *understand* it, it is unlikely to be of much use as a learning resource. Syllable- and word-counts correlate less well with comprehension. (After all, some long words are familiar; many short words aren't.) Comprehension will in any case depend on the relationship between the text and a pupil's prior knowledge. If two texts score identically in terms of quantitative measures of readability and yet one deals with a subject on which the pupil is knowledgeable and one does not, the pupil is likely to understand the former better than the latter.

Many more sophisticated indexes have been developed, but the more sophisticated they are, the more unwieldy they tend to be to use.

The point here is not that quantitative assessments of readability are useless. Rather it is that they need to be used critically. The results they produce need always to be interpreted.

A second option is to assess readability, and understandability, qualitatively. I use the following method. First, read through the text while trying to see it through the eyes of the pupils. Then, consider it from each of the following perspectives:

1. Visual qualities: how reader-friendly are such aspects as layout, line spacing, font size and style, clarity of print, use of symbols and so on?
2. Conceptual qualities: how difficult are the ideas and the logic?
3. Vocabulary: how reader-friendly is the choice of words?
4. Sentence construction: how reader-friendly is the syntax and grammar? Consider, the sequencing of terms, the position of the subject and the verb, the use of subordinate clauses and so on.
5. Genre conventions and discourse structure: how clear will it be to your pupils what type of text this is, how this type of text should be read, how the text is structured and how the reader should move from one unit of the text to the next?

Finally, go back to the text and take an overall view.

This method will help you to make well-informed assessments. It can be time-consuming to apply, though less so with practice. Inevitably, however, the results will be somewhat impressionistic and prone to subjective errors.

Quantitative and qualitative methods, then, each have their strengths and weaknesses. The best solution is to use the two methods in *combination*.

Select two or more textual resources.

1. Assess their readability quantitatively, using one or more of the internet resources cited in the 'Further reading' section at the end of this chapter.
2. Assess their readability qualitatively, using the above method.
3. Consider the quantitative and qualitative findings together. How useful do you find it to combine the two methods?

Design

If you design your own resources, you will want to make them look attractive. This requires more than technical proficiency with word-processing and desktop publishing software. If, like me, you are not blessed with a natural eye for design, I recommend using the principles below. They have been developed by a designer, Robyn Williams, for use by non-designers and are easy to understand, remember and apply.

The first principle is contrast. Williams advocates using *strong* contrast to create interest. If, for example, you intend to differentiate between two segments of text by varying the font size, Williams suggest you do this not by tinkering with point size (merely contrasting, say, 12- and 14-point type) but making the contrast very pronounced. In particular, she suggests that titles should contrast boldly with body text. I find that on an A4 sheet, a title in, say, 48-point type contrasted <u>to</u> text in 12-point, can make a document more arresting.

The second principle is repetition. Repeat certain design elements – colours, for example, or symbols – to bind the document together and create a sense of coherence. This principle can be applied between documents as well as within them. For example, if you are developing a series of worksheets, seek to establish a method of colour-coding so that a certain colour will signify the same thing on each sheet. You might use red to signify 'instruction', say, or 'top tip').

Williams's third principle is alignment. Whenever you add an element to a document, seek to align it with some other element. If, for example, you decide to include a text box on a worksheet – containing, say, examples of key vocabulary – try to align at least one of its edges (perhaps more), either horizontally or vertically, with another line. Learn to look at your document as a potential grid of vertical and horizontal alignments.

The fourth and final principle is proximity. Where two pieces of information are related to each other (the titles of the document and the curriculum unit it belongs to, say), place them close to each other on the page. Where two elements are unrelated, they may be placed far apart.

Bringing it all together

The focus through much of this chapter has been on the work of the teacher. Ultimately what matters, though, is the experience of the learner. It is helpful, therefore, to conclude by developing an overview of how resources involve the learner. Here again the work of the ELT profession is helpful. David Nunan has suggested categorizing resources according to the type of response demanded from the learner.

He proposes three main categories. First, there are resources that pupils are required to process but not to do anything more with. Their processing of the material may require no response at all (e.g. observing) or may require a response of some sort (e.g. ticking a box, raising a hand).

Second, resources may require from the pupil some form of productive work. Nunan identifies two main types of response here. One is straightforward repetition (e.g. the teacher says something, the pupil repeats it). The other involves practising in some way (whether merely working through a drill or some more meaningful practice).

The third type of resource is interactive. Here the pupil has to respond more fully or openly. This might involve real-world responses, such as problem-solving or genuine discussion, or a simulated response (e.g. role play).

Nunan's precise categories are obviously formulated with language teaching in mind. Terms such as 'repetition', 'drill' and 'role play' will apply more usefully in some curricular subjects than others. But in subjects where such specifications are less applicable, it is not difficult to devise one's own typology, substituting more appropriate terms. The key point is the need to consider what each resource requires from the learner. This will help to gauge whether the menu of resources is sufficiently varied and ambitious.

How appropriate are Nunan's categories for your area of teaching? If you had to design an ideal typology for resource use for your own work, what would it look like?

Though I'm reluctant to reduce the content of this chapter to a single sentence, if I had to, it would be:

For each available resource, consider the relationship to the teacher and the type of requirement made of the learner.

Further reading

The chapter entitled 'Developing learning resources' in Yvonne Hillier, *Reflective Teaching in Further and Adult Education* is extremely practical. Much of the advice applies to school contexts too.

Ian McGrath's discussion of ways of using coursebooks is to be found in *Materials Evaluation and Design for Language Teaching*.

Common quantitative measures of readability include those developed by Fry and by Flesch and also the SMOG (Simple Measure of Gobbledygook) index. Straightforward accounts of these are available on the internet, often accompanied by software to enable the assessment of electronic text. At the time of writing (4 August 2008), the entries in Wikipedia (http://en.wikipedia.org) for 'Fry Readability Formula', 'Flesch–Kincaid Readability Tests' and 'SMOG' are helpful, as is the Readability Formulas website (www.readabilityformulas.com). For a thorough and wide-ranging treatment of readability and its assessment, see Jaan Mikk's monograph, *Textbook*.

Robyn Williams, *The Non-designer's Design Book* is a very accessible, very practical and concise guide to design principles.

David Nunan's typology of learner responses is summarized in the chapter on 'process-oriented syllabuses' in *Syllabus Design*.

9

Time

Time is a key variable in teaching. It is, however, more often commented on than properly discussed. To be effective, we need to consider at least three time scales, namely:

1. Time across the year.
2. Time within the week.
3. Time within the lesson.

In school, time clearly does not proceed in undifferentiated fashion throughout the year. Different times of year work in different ways. Various events shape the rhythm of the academic year – exams, vacations, activity days, school visits, report-writing, work experience projects, public events such as public holidays and festivals and even changes in weather and light. Many of these are known about in advance and need, therefore, to be planned around. It's no good complaining, for example, about the sports day 'interrupting' one's schemes of work when in fact the day was listed on the calendar at the start of the year: being interrupted by a known event is simply a sign of poor planning.

It is important to avoid the temptation of allowing seasonal changes to slow the pace of learning. It is very easy, for example, to allow the thought that 'it's nearly the holidays' to become a reason for taking one's foot off the accelerator. If a teacher dissipates the last week of lessons with entertainment activities – showing DVDs and so on – it's no good then saying that the system doesn't allow enough time to cover the course properly or that some topics can't be included in the curriculum because there isn't enough time. The bottom line is that 'it's nearly the holidays' means in fact that it is*n't* the holidays yet.

There can be few people in schools unaware that the time of week makes a difference to activities. We would all, for example, rather teach in the morning than the afternoon. I've found three observations of weekly time to be useful. The first came from a headteacher who demonstrated, with statistics of disciplinary incidents, that pupils' behaviour was at its worst on Thursdays. Get a good night's sleep the night before and plan your lessons extra carefully was the obvious inference. Second (this an observation I have heard attributed to Ludwig Wittgenstein) there are fat days and thin days. Fat days – Monday, Wednesday and Friday – have their own character. The thin days seem merely to fit in between. Certainly I have always found it easier to persuade colleagues to 'fit things in' on their thin days. Third (this cited in a management study, though I fear I do not remember which) different times of week suit different activities. Mondays seem good for crunchy, analytic, thinking and hard decisions; Fridays seem good for creative and people-centred activities.

The third type of time, that is, time within the lesson, will be dealt with in detail below.

No matter which time scale we are thinking on, we need to remember that there are two general kinds of time: objective time, measured by the steady ticking of the chronograph, and subjective time, measured by our feeling. I still recall as a pupil looking out, during one particularly uninspiring lesson, through the north-facing windows on a dreary Monday afternoon in November and thinking that time had actually come to a stop!

This chapter is designed to help you to, in general, control time and use it productively in classroom planning and, in particular, to plan the following aspects of lessons effectively: (a) beginnings of lessons, (b) ends of lessons and (c) the setting of homework.

Getting the timing right

Most novice teachers find time difficult to plan. It is a common experience to find that an activity that one thought might fill an hour's lesson in fact takes only a quarter of the time, while an activity one thought would take 10 min somehow expands to three-quarters of an hour. The more one wants the pupils to slow down or hurry up, the more they seem – quite unconsciously – to do the opposite. Few things induce more panic in a teacher than the realization that the timing is going all wrong.

The bad news is that there is no simple solution to this. What is needed is experience. The more one teaches, the more one learns to gauge these things. But it may well take a thousand lessons or more to develop an internal clock that is at all reliable.

The good news is that though experience is usually required, that is usually *all* that is required. Generally, the more you teach, the more you find the problem goes away.

In the meantime, there are some things you can do to improve your planning. The first is to record the use of time in the classroom. When you have the opportunity to observe other teachers, record how long each activity takes. You may well find the results are not what you expected. Also record time during your own lessons. Every now and then, find a moment to glance at your watch and on each occasion jot down on your lesson plan where you had got to in the lesson. You can then use these records to inform your lesson planning.

The second thing you can do is to think through each activity in advance. Supposing, for example, you decide in your lesson plan that you are going to hand out some resources. Think the activity through in slow motion. Where are the resources kept? Do you, for example, need to allow time to unlock a cupboard? How are you going to give them out? – by walking around the room or by asking pupils to help you? It is often these mundane operations that lead to miscalculations of timing.

Lastly, build some flexibility into your lesson plan. For example, if you think an activity might take 5 min, write '2½–7½ mins' on your plan. You can then plan for best and worse case scenarios.

Rhythm and pace

As we saw above, there is objective time and there is subjective time – and the latter, because it is a matter of impressions, does not move at a constant pace. Your pupils' experience of time is certainly not something you can wholly control. It is, however, something you can influence through good planning.

Especially important here is rhythm. The rhythm of a lesson is partly a function of the pace of teaching. In general, in the profession and in the literature that supports it, pacy teaching is seen as good teaching – the conventional wisdom is 'the pacier, the better'. In general, I think this is correct. Don't give people time to get distracted or to decide that they are bored.

I am not convinced, however, that an unremittingly fast pace is desirable. There is a danger that everyone – teachers and pupils alike – will be worn out by the end of the day. And some types of learning – or type of learner – will benefit from periods of quietness, stillness, reflection and even rumination or meditation. What is undeniable is that the question of pace matters, so it is important to determine the optimum pace for the activity in question.

Rhythm is a function not only of pace, but also of structure. It helps to divide time into chunks, each delimited by milestones. When, at the end of a chunk of time, you reach a milestone, there is a sense of completion and, ideally, achievement. A milestone provides an occasion to say, 'We've done one thing – and now we're moving on.' Without milestones to demarcate our progress, time can seem for all concerned to stretch ahead interminably.

Too often the only milestones provided for pupils on a typical day are those in the school timetable – lunch break, the bell at the end of the lesson and so on. The problem here is that the gaps between – which are often an hour or more – can feel very long, especially to young people. It is useful, therefore, to create clear milestones within lessons – points where you can say, 'We've done X now and we're moving on to Y.'

Try to announce the milestone while an activity still has life in it, rather than when it has started to drag. Doing the former will indicate that you are a purposeful leader; the latter will suggest that things take their own course in your classroom and that you merely respond to them.

Starts of lessons

The most important phase of the lesson is the beginning. One point that has become very clear to me through observation is that it is usually possible to tell early on how successful a lesson is likely to be. If a lesson is going well after 5 min, it is reasonably likely to be going well after 45 – but if all is not well after 5 min, the chances of the lesson finishing well are slim.

Let's clarify the causal relations here. It is easy to assume that (a) the way that a lesson begins and (b) the way that it proceeds are both merely reflections of the quality of the teacher's practice. That is, a good teacher is likely to achieve both (a) and (b). The problem with this line of reasoning lies in the word 'merely': the way that the lesson proceeds is not the product only of the quality of the teacher, but also of the start of the lesson. That is, the way a lesson starts becomes itself a factor in how the lesson subsequently develops: it has a multiplier effect. The good news here is that, because the beginnings of lessons have a disproportionate effect, you can improve the overall quality of your lessons simply by improving the way you start them.

> I once worked in a department where we arranged to observe and record the way that each teacher began lessons. I found the experience very instructive. I particularly remember observing one lesson. The teacher was a little late arriving to unlock the door to let the pupils in. He wasn't very late – but the extra few seconds were enough to make the start feel less than snappy. Each subsequent process – the business of pupils sitting down, taking off their coats, getting out their pens and books, putting their bags away – seemed to take longer than it should. While this was going on (or not), the teacher was largely ignoring the class. Instead he was rootling around among piles of folders, looking for the resources he needed. A few pupils drifted in late.

My observation sheet required me to log the precise times for the following:

1. When the teachers arrived.
2. When pupils entered the room.
3. When pupils were sitting down.
4. When the teacher formally began the lesson.
5. When pupils started work on a task.

In this class each of these took longer than they needed to. For example, it took over 10% of the total lesson time to reach (4) and over a third of the lesson to reach (5). Revealingly, the teacher was surprised by the timings – he hadn't realized things had taken so long.

Once the lesson did get under way, progress was slowed further by poor concentration from pupils, some of whom distracted each other. The single most useful lesson for me as an observer was that I noticed that the bulk of the class seemed to me to arrive in a reasonably positive mood. By about 20 min into the lesson, however, some of these seemingly benign pupils were unsettled and clearly not in learning mode. It was very evident that the slow start was the cause of the problem. A number of pupils had simply concluded that nothing very much was happening and become bored and then restless (as indeed did I!)

Note that the start of the lesson wasn't *awful*. It wasn't mayhem, it wasn't a riot. It was just very slow. And that was enough to ensure that what could have been a successful lesson certainly wasn't.

Ends of lessons

Ends of lessons may not be as powerful as the beginnings, but they are significant. This is not least because, if a lesson ends well, it makes a successful start to the next lesson with the same class more likely. The main avoidable cause of a poor ending is failure to anticipate how long the closing process will take. Such activities as wrapping up the teaching and learning, collecting work and resources, ensuring pupils pack away their own possessions, cleaning and tidying and leaving in orderly fashion each take time.

Note that it is better to finish a little early than a little late. The latter nearly always leads to some mixture of anxiety, resentment and problems further down the line (a delayed start to the next class, for example). I have noticed that some good teachers make a habit of regularly finishing lessons just a little early. This allows a minute for sitting in a composed, tidy, classroom. The same teachers tend to use this time for certain routines – informal ones such as off-task, social chit-chat with pupils or formal ones such as word games. It has always seemed to me that everyone appreciates, and gains from, a relaxed ending.

It is important, therefore, to apply the general techniques outlined above (see 'Getting the timing right'). If you find that the ending of a lesson does go awry, it is important afterwards to reflect on why it did so. Did you take your eye off the clock? Were your instructions unclear? Identify the reason and then consciously avoid the problem next time round by adapting your lesson plan.

Setting homework

A common problem of time management in the classroom concerns the setting of homework. It is easy to underestimate how long it takes. This always leads to a dilemma. Either (a) you give more time to it than you had planned, which puts pressure on the next activity or (b) you rush the process, which leads to problems when you come to collect the work (you find either it hasn't been done or it has been done poorly or incorrectly). On balance (a) is usually preferable to (b), but isn't an option if it's the end of the lesson.

The key is to recognize that 'setting homework' does not equate with 'saying what the homework is'. Setting homework requires you both to inform pupils what the task is and to explain it, to

invite and answer queries and to ensure that the pupils record the
task correctly. Often the final stage requires some checking on
your part. Properly to set homework, therefore, takes longer than
merely saying what homework is.

Setting homework is often left until the end of the lesson.
That is often a mistake. If you find that the process begins to
take longer than expected, you have no room for flexibility.
Moreover, leaving homework until the end can devalue it: it
can make homework seem like an add-on or an afterthought.
Instead, plan to set the homework early on in the lesson.
Implicitly this will send the message that you have thought the
homework through and that you see it as an integral part of
your teaching.

Above I outlined the following thresholds to achieve as quickly as
possible at the start of a lesson:

1. The time by which the teacher has arrived.
2. The time by which the pupils have entered the room.
3. The time by which pupils are sitting down.
4. The time by which the teacher has formally begun the lesson.
5. The time by which pupils are on task.

You can use this framework to help improve your lesson planning.

(A) If you have the opportunity to observe other teachers:
    (i) design an observation sheet and use it to record the times
    for (1) to (5) above. Also jot down any key points you notice;
    (ii) then reflect on your findings and ask yourself what could
    be done to arrive at each threshold time sooner.
(B) If you have the opportunity to be observed, ask someone else
    to carry out activity (A) in one of your lessons.

Over the period of a week, try – though not at the expense of interrupting the flow of your lessons – regularly to record the times you
achieve for each of the above thresholds and use these to inform
your planning.

Bringing it all together

It is possible to divide types of time into three broad categories:

1. Time spent on learning activities.
2. Time spent on support activities.
3. Other uses of time.

Type (2) includes all those processes occurring during the lesson that do not constitute learning activities, but which are necessary in order for the learning activities to get done. They include, for example, pupils obtaining resources – textbooks, paper and so on – that they need during the lesson. Type (3) includes activities such as getting distracted, misbehaving and discussing subjects irrelevant to the learning activity.

The aim is obviously to maximize (1) and to minimize (2) and (3). Gains in (1) can often be achieved simply by giving more forethought to (2). It is extraordinary how much the time taken up with, say, giving out some worksheets can vary between classrooms. When planning, therefore, it is useful to review the common routines in your classroom. Examples might include:

– Giving out resources.
– Collecting resources.
– Rearranging space, for example to enable a group discussion to take place.
– Tidying up.

In each case, consider how to streamline the activity. Remember that there is only one of you! This often becomes a constraint in the classroom – you can't do everything yourself quickly enough. Give some thought, therefore, to how you can involve other people – especially pupils – in the routines. Having decided how you want a certain routine to be performed, explain it and then ensure it happens. Even if you have to appear finicky at first, time spent getting routines established is time well spent (or, rather, invested).

103

Though I'm reluctant to reduce the content of this chapter to a single sentence, if I had to, it would be:

Plan the rhythm of each lesson.

Further reading

Most teachers recognize that time is an important factor in education and one often hears comments about time. Strangely the professional literature does not properly reflect this. Many guides and textbooks contain little or no advice on the issue. One exception is Michael Marland's *Craft of the Classroom*. This is a classic short guide to practical aspects of teaching. It is particularly strong on the need to establish routines in the classroom.

10

Space

Space is something that people in schools often feel very strongly about. Managers, teachers and pupils often exhibit territorial behaviour. Notably, managers seem – to judge by where they choose to locate their offices – keen to ensure that pupils rarely get near to them! In schools, such issues as who sits where and who is allowed to go where often prove contentious. Yet it's difficult for a teacher who wishes to make optimum use of space to find much guidance on the issue.

Broadly, there are three types of relationship between the teaching space and one's own teaching. (1) You can use it conventionally and unreflectively, in which case space will be largely inert. It will function neither positively nor negatively in your teaching. (2) You can be careless over space, in which case it can rapidly begin to contribute negatively to the learning in your lessons. Or (3) you can see space as a resource to be used decisively and even creatively – in which case it can become a positive force.

This chapter has been designed to help you, in general, to make optimal use of the space available to you and, in particular, to decide how to manage space in terms of (a) layout, (b) movement and (c) the condition of the fabric.

Classroom layouts

One encounters many layouts in classrooms. Sometimes – in laboratories and ICT rooms, for example – they are very rigid.

105

Even in less rigid spaces, factors such as room dimensions, types of furniture and numbers of pupils constrain the way space can be used. Usually, though, there is at least a degree of flexibility and so the question of which layout to use becomes pertinent.

Each layout has its own advantages and disadvantages. One very common layout, especially in secondary schools, is rows. Here the main organizing principle is that desks are arranged parallel to the front wall, with pupils sitting behind them facing the board at the front.

This layout has some obvious advantages. It focuses attention on the teacher and board or screen at the front. It is, therefore, well suited to presentations and didactic teaching. It helps the teacher with surveillance and it provides obvious ways of separating pupils from each other. It provides clear options for where to sit pupils with special needs concerning hearing or eyesight. It can – especially if there are breaks in the rows – make the giving out and collection of resources straightforward. It provides some flexibility – the class can usually turn to pair work with ease. And it is a familiar format that conforms to expectations.

But organization by rows also has disadvantages. It has unhelpful associations of Victorian-style regimentation – though I suspect this bothers educators more than pupils. It makes discussion other than in pairs difficult. Organization by rows is one of the main reasons why so-called whole-class discussions so often turn into teacher-dominated events in which the pupils rarely respond directly to each other. The layout can encourage teachers to stay at the front of the class so that the back of the classroom becomes a rarely visited space. It is difficult to combine this layout with a principle of equality of opportunity, since some seats tend to be treated as peripheral. And, finally, it is undeniably boring.

Another common format, especially in primary schools, is nests. Here tables are arranged into groups of two or three. This too has certain advantages. It is obviously well suited to small group work. It can be used to aid differentiation, with different types of work going on on different tables.

However, the layout also has some disadvantages. It can make whole-class teaching more difficult, especially if pupils are required not only to face the front but also to take notes. It can also make it easy for pupils to become distracted – and to distract each other – during individual or pair work.

A third common format is the horseshoe, in which desks are arranged approximately in a U-shape, with a gap at the front. This can make whole class discussion more open, with more direct interaction between pupils. It can, provided the room is not too narrow, be arranged so that pupils can see the front of the room fairly well, so it gains some of the advantages of the row format. But it can lead to pupils who are sitting opposite each other distracting each other. And it can make small group work difficult.

In a horseshoe it is important that the middle is open, so that the teacher can approach pupils and talk to each one face-to-face. This, however uses up valuable space. It can also create a cavernous feel, in which people on each side feel further from the other side than is in fact the case.

Which layout one opts for will depend on factors such as the size, shape and design of the room, the type of furniture and the number of pupils. One crucial consideration is the type of teaching and learning you plan for your lessons. So far as possible, you want to choose the layout most conducive to your style of work.

Yet, oddly, many teachers fail to do this. One social psychologist, Nigel Hastings, researched classrooms in many primary schools. He found that layout and work style were often ill-matched. Often, rooms were arranged according to the nesting principle, yet the work that pupils were most often required to do – involving individual study and whole-class teaching – was least suited to that format. His argument was a simple one – that many teachers could raise standards of learning in their room by rearranging the furniture within it to suit their teaching styles.

In *Guerilla Guide to Teaching*, Sue Cowley strongly advocates giving careful thought and implementing decisions on layout before the start of the school year. She points out that doing so can help the teacher to take charge, establish a style, become familiar with a room and feel confident in it. And, as Sue says, 'It's actually good fun setting up the classroom exactly the way you want it' (p. 152).

Who sits where?

Questions of who does what, where can easily become contentious. If you wish to avoid this happening, the best technique is anticipation: establish beforehand what the conventions are about space in your classroom.

One key question is who sits where. This raises a number of issues. To what extent, for example, does one want to mix different groups – socio-economic groups, ethnic groups, the sexes, aptitude groups and so on? Such considerations raise in turn the question of who decides. Pupils will often want to make the decision where to sit and some will challenge the teacher's right to decide otherwise. And teachers are sometimes shy of being directive about seating. One can see the point. When teaching or training adults, for example, I might well be wary of being directive on this issue. It is not surprising, therefore, if the closer to adulthood the pupils become, the more they expect the same 'right'.

There are, however, good grounds for teachers to be directive. Consider the analogy of time. Teachers are rarely shy when it comes to directing the use of time. What subject pupils are studying, what activities they are engaged in, how long they have for them – such decisions are routinely made by teachers.

The key consideration here is surely learning. If one directs the use of time in order to encourage optimal learning, why should the use of space be any different? Though there can certainly be benefits to allowing pupils to make decisions over space, the drawback is that the criterion of 'what is best for learning?' is unlikely to be paramount for pupils. Social considerations will tend to predominate. And with these comes peer pressure, so that it is not at all certain that in a non-directive classroom each pupil will end up sitting where they really wish to be.

It is best to decide the principle of organization before the first class of the year and to begin by implementing it. Be aware, however, that this does not mean that you need maintain the same pattern throughout the year. While constant changing can prove unsettling and produce friction, making changes for particular purposes can be beneficial. It may be, for example, that for a particular piece of work it would be advantageous to move pupils into single-sex (or, for that matter, mixed) groups. The more one can present such decisions as driven by questions of learning, the more one can remove the sense of ego from the equation.

When I was a pupil, there was one teacher whose classes I particularly liked. One of the main reasons was that his lessons produced lively discussions in which pupils contributed fully. One day I tried to work out why the discussion in this class was so much more lively than in others. There were several reasons. The teacher's sense of humour certainly helped. But I decided that one reason was the layout of the room. In particular, the layout was asymmetrical. There were some rows, but they were of different lengths. And there were also some tables, including the one I sat at, that were side-on. Somehow it allowed different characters to adopt different spaces – and different roles in the discussion. Interestingly, the next year the same class had the same teacher in a different room. The desks were arranged symmetrically in rows. The lessons were still good – but the discussions were not as lively as before.

Most classrooms I have seen have been arranged symmetrically – or at least as symmetrically as the room allows. Is this really the product of conscious thought? Or is it just the tyranny of symmetry?

Conventions

When planning classroom activities, bear in mind that movement in the classroom can produce friction. The more everyone in your classroom knows in advance where things are and what the norms are about who uses what space under what circumstances, the more one can avoid distraction. For example, a boy in your class needs some rough paper: does he know where it's kept? Can he help himself? Devote time to establishing conventions. You may wish, for example, to establish a 'quiet corner' or a 'reading table' or whatever. The more upfront and consistent you are about the conventions, the smoother the progress of the lesson is likely to be.

Wherever possible, delegate responsibility. Let people perform simple tasks for themselves; appoint monitors or ask for volunteers to keep any eye on things – to keep pencils sharpened, blinds at the right height and so on.

Fabric

Deterioration of the fabric of the school tends to escalate. Graffiti leads to more graffiti. More graffiti leads to damage. Damage leads to breakages. Before long, someone burns the school down. You need, therefore, to be vigilant. If you notice a problem, ensure it is dealt with. Don't turn a blind eye to minor problems, such as graffiti on desks. Deal with the problem – and be seen to deal with it.

The good news here is that it is possible to get into a positive cycle, where improvements make deterioration less likely to occur in future. In one school I worked in, the rooms my department worked in were in poor condition. Years ago, when two schools had merged, things had been dumped around the department rather haphazardly. The department had a poor grip on its resources. Some were stored in a corridor where they were easily damaged or stolen. Others were difficult to find. We had no inventory. When the summer holidays came around, a group of us decided to devote several days to sorting out the resources and the physical environment of the department. We audited our resources and arranged them so that they could be kept securely and retrieved easily. We filled a large skip with junk.

While I didn't relish spending several fine summer days indoors, clearing up, I never regretted it. When I returned to school in September, the benefits – both practical and aesthetic – of our sort-out put a spring in my step. The point that interested me most – and the reason I include the anecdote here – was the reaction of the pupils. It was very clear that they noticed, that they thought it significant and that they approved. 'Had a bit of a clear out, haven't you, sir? It needed it – it was a right dump!' The pupils derived a clear message: 'Things are on the way up here'.

Your key ally in the fight to maintain the fabric of the space around you is the site manager, whose co-operation is often the difference between getting things done – and done promptly – or not. Teachers are not always good at managing their relationship with the site manager, who can easily feel ignored, taken for granted, unfairly put upon or patronized. It is a good idea ('good' in more ways than one) to devote time and care to developing this relationship from the moment one starts to work in a school. Take time – at the right moments – to talk, to listen and to acknowledge.

If you are able to observe other teachers, try logging their use of space. At regular intervals over a certain length of time (say, every 30 s for 15 min), record where the teacher is standing or sitting.

On another occasion you can instead log the teacher's interactions with pupils. It is difficult to do this fully, because some interactions – eye contact – can be difficult to capture. You will need, therefore, to decide how to define 'interaction' and to restrict your observation to types that are easy to log.

After the lesson, reflect on your findings. How did the teacher use (or fail to use) space? How did the experience of pupils in different spaces vary? Do you think learning in the classroom could be improved by a different use of space? If so, how could that be facilitated?

Display

One of the most positive contributions you can make to the physical environment is to mount and maintain good displays on the walls in and around your classroom. Doing so is doubly beneficial: the display constitutes a good use of space in its own right and also sends the right messages about caring for, and taking pride in, the space around us.

When designing a display, consider three elements. First, ensure that it is attractive to the eye and enhances the visual environment. Second, ensure the values it reflects are appropriate for the classroom. Third, try to make the display interactive. In particular, try to design it as a resource to draw on in your teaching.

In my experience, there are a number of simple conventions that, if followed, make for a decorative display. Use large lettering for headings and labels. Remember it needs to be clear not only from where you are standing while mounting the display, but also from the opposite side of the classroom. Decide how large such lettering needs to be and then make it even larger. People tend, intuitively, to use upper case lettering for headings. This is a mistake: lower case lettering, because it includes letters with headers and tails, is in fact easier to decipher at a distance. Use sans-serif font for the headings. Seek to align the elements of a display. The more each vertical and horizontal edge aligns with another such edge, the greater will be the sense of organization and harmony – though of course you can also create interest by placing some components so that they deliberately subvert the pattern you have created. Leave plenty of space between components. It is a common fault of classroom displays that they seek to cram too much in, with the result that the components jostle each other for attention. Keep refreshing the displays so that they don't become faded or frayed.

There are also some simple conventions for selection of material for display. When selecting pupils' work, reward effort as well as achievement. The danger of not doing so is that some children's work will get consistently overlooked. Try as much as possible, at least over time, to ensure that displays represent the balance of the curriculum. One question to consider is the balance of pupils' work against other kinds of display material. The educational advantages of displaying pupils' own work (and involving them in the process of mounting the display) are obvious. However, one sometimes encounters an orthodoxy based on the view that only pupils' work should be displayed. For example, in an otherwise excellent section on displays in *Teaching 3–8*, Mark O'Hara writes, 'If the aim is to motivate pupils, then it ought to be the children's work, not the teacher's, that is displayed' (p. 84). That 'if' is important: there are other reasons for mounting displays, such as introducing new kinds of stimuli. If too rigidly enforced, the view that 'display = pupils' work' can lead to same-y environments and missed opportunities. I have always enjoyed displays that juxtapose pupils' work with other resources (professionally produced posters, for example) so that the two types of material seem to interact with, or comment on, each other.

Bringing it all together

'Do you ever walk into a classroom and *not* change the furniture around?' a student in an adult class once asked me. She was speaking tongue-in-cheek, but behind her quip was a serious point. The rooms I taught evening classes in were used during the day for larger, secondary, classes in a different curriculum area. Their layouts were inappropriate for the evening classes. And, in any case, I varied the layouts for those classes according to the type of work we were doing.

Several key points about space are summed up in this unremarkable cameo. In particular:

- Different layouts have different potentials.
- The teacher needs to take control of the space and decide how to use it to optimize learning.

If you teach in a space that has at least some flexibility and yet you never think to vary its layout, that is probably a warning sign: either the layout will at times be less than optimal for the work you are doing or the teaching and learning in your classroom is becoming rather same-y. I have always liked to think of shaping the layout of a room as a kind of choreography. It would be an exaggeration to say that classroom layout actually scripts the lessons that take place in it, but it certainly helps to shape them.

It is important to give some forethought to the question of how to convert one layout to another. In the evening class example, I had the luxury of arriving well before the start of the lesson and even finding that one or two of the early arrivals would quite willingly help with moving chairs around. Often, though, the business of changing layouts is complicated by the presence of a few dozen young people. One needs, therefore, to have thought through how change can be accomplished safely and efficiently.

One final point about space – and perhaps the most important: when planning, take care to allow time to ensure that you leave teaching spaces the way your colleagues would wish to find them – if you wish to retain their good will and your professional reputation, that is.

Though I'm reluctant to reduce the content of this chapter to a single sentence, if I had to, it would be:

> Prepare the space you teach in and the use you and your pupils will make of it.

Further reading

Sue Cowley provides a chapter on 'Setting up your room' in *Guerilla Guide to Teaching: The Definitive Resource for New Teachers*.

Nigel Hastings' research, discussed above, is presented in Nigel Hastings and Karen Chantrey Wood, *Re-Organizing Primary Classroom Learning*.

For a sensible and concise guide to classroom display, including a practical checklist, see Mark O'Hara, *Teaching 3–8*. The entry on 'Displays' in Lyn Overall and Margaret Sangster, *Primary Teacher's Handbook* also provides concise advice, supported by a list of strategies relating both to short- and medium-term planning.

11

Language

Language is involved, one way or another, in most – arguably all – teaching and learning activities. Teachers talk to their classes, pupils read worksheets, discuss DVDs and so on. And the same is true of assessment activities: pupils complete exercises, give talks, write answers to examination questions and so on. This is true not only of the obviously linguistic subjects, such as English and Modern Foreign Languages, but also of subjects elsewhere in the curriculum – Science, Art and Physical Education, for example.

That all curriculum subjects inter-relate with language may seem obvious, even banal, when stated. Yet it's frequently forgotten – or not even recognized in the first place. The damage done by failing either to recognize or to remember this point can be quite severe. Consider the implications of the fact that most learning is mediated by language. For example, if a pupil does not learn a topic very effectively, there might be several causes. There might be a problem with the topic or the pupil – or it might just be that there is a problem with the language being used to mediate between the two. Before we rush to the conclusion that the topic is too difficult or that the pupil is too 'dim', or has special needs, or whatever, we need to consider whether linguistic changes would do the trick.

A similar point applies to assessment. One science teacher asked me to review the written assignments that he gave his pupils. I asked him whether he'd ever tried doing any of the tasks himself. He hadn't. I asked him which he would find most demanding. It was very clear that for the assignments he chose, the demands would not tax his scientific knowledge. He knew his subject inside-out. It was the linguistic challenges he didn't fancy. And some of our pupils find themselves in that situation day after day.

The moral should be clear: any teacher who cares neither about how much pupils learn nor how much learning they can demonstrate can afford to neglect language in their lesson planning! This chapter takes more positive stance: it is designed to help you incorporate language into lesson planning by considering some of the main ways in which language and learning interact.

Principles of language development

Language acquisition and language development have become subjects in their own right within Linguistics. The volume of research is now such that, if working alone, even a world expert would not be able to keep abreast of it all. This can be daunting for teachers, who happen to have a rather demanding day job to attend to. Fortunately, on a pragmatic level, a few straightforward principles can take us quite a long way. Four principles, to be precise.

The first is that pupils' language development (and hence their learning) will progress best when modes of language are interrelated. Imagine, for example, trying to do an interview if you had never heard one. Or trying to write a letter if you'd never seen one. It is commonly said that there are four modes of language and these may be categorized according to whether they are:

(a) spoken or written down;
(b) receptive or productive.

This is summarized in Table 11.1.

Table 11.1   Modes of language

	Receptive	Productive
Speech	Listening	Speaking
Text	Reading	Writing

As can clearly be seen from the examples mentioned above, our language development tends to proceed most smoothly when these language modes are all mixed in together, so that one can apply in one mode what one has learnt in another. This might sound obvious – yet on several occasions, at various levels of education, I've had conversations along the lines of the following:

Teacher: My students are no good at writing essays.
Me: How many essays have you given them to read?
Teacher: None. I only ask them to write them.

– at which point, some look sheepish, but others still don't get it.

Problems can arise, therefore, from a failure to integrate language modes in the classroom – more often than not, a failure to incorporate reading and pupils' speaking into schemes of work. The good news is the corollary: when the various modes of language are fully integrated into learning, the result can be exciting. Pupils start to transfer knowledge from one mode to another. They may find, for example, that having tried out ideas in pair or group discussion, they become easier to express and develop on paper. Or they may start to borrow for their own writing layouts and formats that they have read in print. In *Learning about Writing*, Pam Czerniewksa gives the example of a teacher who displayed musical notation on the walls of a nursery classroom and found that children started to incorporate the symbols in their writing, almost by a process of osmosis.

The second principle follows closely from the first. It is that language development will progress best when critical and creative work are combined. Here I'm using the word 'critical' broadly. I don't intend the word simply in the sense of literary or artistic criticism, nor in its everyday sense of making negative comments. Rather, we are referring to any process of examining, analysing, or discussing pre-existing texts or artefacts, whether they be stories, articles, web pages, television programmes or whatever. Similarly the word 'creative' here goes beyond (though it includes) artistic endeavours such as drawing or drama. It includes all original enterprises on the part of pupils – giving presentations, conducting surveys, designing experiments and so on. 'Critical' and 'creative' thus include activities from all parts of the curriculum and all phases of education.

Suppose, for example, you wish pupils to use tabular material in their writing. It will be helpful in that case if they look at how some other writers have done so. Let them read such material and help them to learn from it by noticing specific features and analysing good and bad points. Often the sequence runs, critical work first, creative work second. But the sequence needn't run that way round. Giving pupils an opportunity to do a creative task can be effective: it can create a context for the critical work and help pupils to relate new material to their existing knowledge.

The third principle is that language development occurs over time and is frequently a long-term process. This requires the teacher to look ahead and consider what demands on pupils' language will be made, both later in the year and also in subsequent years or phases. It also requires the teacher to look back at what pupils have or haven't learnt in the past – again, not only within the year, but also in previous years. Official documents such as syllabus outlines are of limited use here, since they show only what the pupil was *supposed* to have experienced and learnt, which may be very different from the actuality. Pupil records and, especially, examples of the pupils' work are likely to be more enlightening.

The third principle requires two qualities on the part of the teacher, namely patience and confidence. Largely for its own purposes, bureaucracy in education puts a great stress on short-term measurable outcomes. In the ideal bureaucratic vision, we can identify and assess learning outcomes by the end of each lesson. Often there are indeed such outcomes – and that is fine. But it is a mistake to believe that learning is *always* like that.

Language development can be a subtle and unpredictable process. I challenge anyone who doubts that to spend a while writing an account of how their own linguistic ability developed: how did they learn to, for example, write an essay, give a presentation, or learn from a textbook? As a teacher, one needs to persist, doing the things that make for linguistic development in the long term, even when there is a lack of comforting short-term data.

The fourth principle is that both procedural and declarative knowledge matter here. A pupil may know how to perform certain linguistic activities effectively – for example, writing a list, taking turns in a discussion – that is, the pupil possesses relevant procedural knowledge. And a pupil might know (declaratively, this is) that, for example, a certain phrase is slangy, that letters usually begin with a greeting ('Dear . . .') or that non-fiction books often have an index at the back.

Though these two types of knowledge often overlap, they are by no means co-extensive. For example, you may know full well (declaratively) that a newspaper article needs a good headline without being able (procedurally) to write one. You may know how (procedurally) to write good dialogue without knowing (declaratively) what 'dialogue' is. Once when a colleague kindly complimented me on my 'sandwiching technique' I hadn't a clue what she meant: I had learnt that it is often most effective to deliver a negative comment between two positives without knowing that the technique had a name – and I'm not even sure I was conscious of it as a technique. I'd just learnt to do it.

Though declarative and procedural knowledge are not co-extensive, they do often inform each other. My colleague might not have been able to teach me instantly what 'sandwiching technique' was if I hadn't already been doing it. Equally, teaching someone – on a training course, say – what sandwiching technique is may encourage them to use it. So we should extend our fourth principle to say, not only that there are both declarative and procedural types of linguistic knowledge but also that it is helpful to develop them in tandem.

To see how these principles may be applied in planning, let's consider an example from our notional course on Architecture. In a town near where I live, a proposal has recently been developed to build a new hotel to be sited in a road that is predominantly residential. The proposal is controversial. The developers argue that the hotel will raise the quantity and quality of accommodation available in the town, attracting more visitors and providing jobs. Opponents argue that the site is inappropriate and the character of the area will be spoilt. Let's suppose that we wanted our pupils to explore this issue and that the main assessment task will be to write a letter, designed to contribute to the debate, to the local newspaper.

One could, of course, just set the task. Some pupils may be able to complete the task very well without further ado – though whether they would produce the best work is open to question. And other pupils would certainly struggle. So, first, let's apply the principle that our planning should integrate the modes of language experienced by the pupils. Listening activities could be provided by, for example, pupils interviewing local residents. Perhaps some of the interviews could be recorded and played in class. In addition, the pupils could listen to each other discuss the proposal – informally in pairs or groups, more formally in a simulated meeting. In addition, the teacher could model various forms of discourse by, for example, drafting simulated comments from various local interest groups. All of this listening activity provides pupils with exposures to the range of vocabulary, grammatical structures and tones that they could employ in their own writing.

Experience of speech can be provided, as we have just seen, through both informal discussion and simulated presentations. Experience of reading may be gained by providing examples of press coverage and passages from actual or simulated documentation. All of this will provide pupils with an opportunity to explore and develop their ideas and in particular, to formulate those ideas in language before they turn to the final assessment task.

To some extent, the second principle – that creative and critical work should be combined – has in this example already been fulfilled: pupils have critically examined a range of opinion and then created their own texts. One could add to the creative element by asking them to generate ideas for alternative uses for the proposed site or alternative sites for the proposed building.

We can apply the third principle by looking back to see what previous curriculum experience may be drawn on. Note that this need not be closely related to the topic. There is potential to draw on pupils' experience of genres such as letter writing, interviewing and debating. The teacher can help pupils to build a bridge between their previous learning and the present task, for example by asking them to reflect on the work they produced earlier in the curriculum. The teacher can also help pupils to develop, by targeting areas for improvement or teaching skills that haven't been developed before.

The fourth principle can be applied by, for example, formally teaching examples of vocabulary (e.g. 'site', 'location', 'economy', 'employment', 'regeneration', 'impact', 'interests') and grammatical structures ('This assumes . . .', 'We submit . . .' etc.). This will help to develop declarative knowledge to complement the procedural knowledge gained through performing the various development or assessment tasks.

Consider an assessment task in a course you teach and plan a sequence of work that incorporates the four principles of:

1. integrating speaking, listening, reading and writing;
2. combining critical and creative work;
3. articulating with pupils' long-term development;
4. incorporating procedural and declarative knowledge.

Listening

Listening tends to be treated in school as if it were a transparent activity. We tend to look right through it. We assume that listening is something that pupils can and should do. We become aware of listening most when it clearly isn't happening, at which point our responses are likely to major on complaints ('Why on earth can't they listen?') and admonition ('Listen! I've told you to listen!')

Some teachers do have conscious strategies for developing pupils' listening. In my experience, such expertise is most often to be found among teachers of foreign languages and music. But often very little attention is given to how to develop pupils' listening capacity and ensure effective listening. Of the various language modes, it is the development of listening that is the least articulated.

To develop pupils' listening, consider first the role of time and space. Seek to ensure that you do not unduly extend the attention span required. As we saw in Chapter 9, it helps here to be aware of how much time activities – such as the teacher addressing the class – actually take. What you may think of as 'a few minutes explanation' can easily turn into a discourse of ten or fifteen minutes. In your lesson plans, try to 'chunk' your presentations into manageable spans, so that you can finish each chunk before attention starts to wane. This will enable you and the class to get into a positive cycle of developing their listening and may enable you over time to gradually extend the attention span required.

Plan your use of space to enhance listening. Consider which way pupils will be facing and what the acoustics of the room are like (the aim should always be to speak somewhat louder than the volume required simply to be heard). Remember that listening in class is a multimodal activity – and not only for those pupils who may rely on lip-reading. Body language, facial expressions and eye contact all play an important role. It is helpful to reflect on the difference, according to actors, between acting for film and acting on stage. Gesture and expression on film, where the camera can zoom in, may be subtle; in an auditorium, they will need to be more pronounced. Teaching in class is much more like acting on stage than on film. Seek, therefore, to develop a repertoire of emphatic gestures and expressions that can't be missed. These may even be somewhat exaggerated – in my experience, pupils seem to remember and respond to teachers with distinctive styles of expression! Do not be afraid to practise your repertoire, with the aid of a good mirror, at home – you won't be the only teacher to do this, though of course you may wish to ensure that you are alone at the time!

Two features are central to the development of a successful listener: the provision of rich aural experiences and the encouragement of active listening. Most teachers do make an effort to provide a stimulating *visual* environment by, for example, decorating the classroom with displays. The aural environment, however, may be much less stimulating – often with a narrow range of voices predominating. In the digital age, this is inexcusable: the internet makes a huge social, geographical and historical range of voices readily accessible, as well as all kinds of other sounds – from the sounds of crowds or wildlife to those of steam engines or gunfire.

Active listening may be developed by specifying the operations for pupils to perform on the material you wish them to listen to. Vague instructions ('listen carefully'; 'take notes') do little to develop pupils' capacity to listen. More productive strategies include:

- giving pupils beforehand questions you expect them to be able to answer as a result of their listening;
- asking pupils to listen out for examples of particular themes;
- completing report forms, structured for selecting and collecting information (e.g. using boxes labelled 'arguments for' and 'arguments against') – perhaps with a defined number of outcomes for each component of the report.

It is useful when designing listening activities to consider the kinds of listening involved. A fourfold typology, outlined by Andrew Pollard in *Reflective Teaching*, is helpful here. The four types of listening, as characterized by Pollard (pp. 306–7), are:

1. interactive listening – where the role of speaker and listener changes rapidly and pupils need to develop the art of turn-taking;
2. reactive listening – where pupils are required to follow and 'take in' an exposition, where the emphasis of the listening should be on following the meaning of the speaker;
3. discriminative listening – where pupils are required to identify, and discriminate between, sounds (e.g. phonemes or musical notes);
4. appreciative listening – for example, listening to a narrative or a rhythmical text such as a song or a poem.

In classrooms, pupils' listening is frequently assessed informally ('you need to listen more carefully'; 'you're not listening'). Often, however, there is a lack of formal assessment. Though there may be exceptions (notably in foreign language lessons), in general pupils' reading comprehension is likely to be assessed formally much more frequently than their aural comprehension. There is a danger here that pupils will infer from the hidden curriculum that accurate, careful listening is much less important.

It is not difficult to design formal assessment tasks for aural comprehension. These may simply be more controlled, standardized versions of the type of active listening tasks outlined above. It is often helpful to provide questions or exercises that are stepped, so that pupils progress – perhaps through listening to the selected material a number of times – from (a) factual recall questions to (b) those requiring inference (listening between the lines, as it were) and then to (c) evaluative questions, where pupils are required to arrive at some sort of assessment, judgement or decision relating to the material.

Reflect on a course that you teach. Consider what opportunities there may be for enriching your pupils' aural curriculum. Seek to identify some readily available resources.

For one of these resources, design a formal assessment task. Seek to include factual, inferential and evaluative questions or exercises. Consider (a) how often the pupils will listen to the resource you have selected and (b) at what point in the activity you will introduce the questions or exercises.

Talk

We use talk in two ways – as a means of conveying thought that has already been formulated and, alternatively, as a way of formulating our thinking in the first place. It is helpful, therefore, to distinguish between pupil talk as a product and pupil talk as a process.

Both kinds of talk are important and need to be developed. But we need to remember that they can be very different. With some forms of talk-as-product – a rehearsed speech, for example – it may be reasonable to ask pupils to aspire to clear enunciation, standard grammar, logically shaped argument and so on. But where talk is functioning more formatively, as process, such expectations may be unreasonable. When transcripts are made of informal discussions of this type, they look very peculiar: grammatical forms are often non-standard, slang may feature strongly, clauses may change direction or be left incomplete. This is entirely natural, yet for teachers who lack confidence in the value of talk-as-process it is easy when overhearing snippets of pair or small group discussion to infer that nothing of value is happening. When planning spoken activities, therefore, it is important to be clear what the purpose of each activity is and not to assess the activity by inappropriate criteria.

Formulating thought through speech can be a highly educational activity. We need, therefore, to ensure that our lesson planning allows time to accommodate this activity. Classroom observation often reveals that pupils on average say very little (on task, at any rate!) during lessons – and typically less than their teachers estimate to be the case. It is easy to see how this comes about. Consider, for example, a one hour lesson in which 20 minutes is given to whole class discussion. If the pattern of the discussion runs teacher–pupil–teacher–pupil, teacher talk may take up half that time. If there is a class of 30 pupils, this allows an average of no more than 20 seconds per pupil. And if the discussion is dominated by a few pupils, it may well be that the average (in the sense of median) pupil in the class says nothing at all! Clearly there is a need for pair and small group discussion.

This is not to imply that lesson plans should have no room for whole class discussions. Far from it. Such discussion is, however, difficult to do well. All too often, well intentioned invitations from the teachers ('I want to know what you think'; 'Let's hear from someone who hasn't spoken yet') fail to elicit the desired response. Whole class discussion benefits from being planned. In my experience, the advice that Alan Howe provides in *Expanding Horizons: Teaching and Learning through Whole Class Discussion* is very productive. Howe advocates preparing pupils for whole class discussion through a series of stages.

For example, the process may begin with pair work. Talk in pairs, Howe notes, has several useful functions. It may help pupils to clarify material, to revise work, to plan a method for approaching a problem or to generate questions. Discussion may then proceed to small groups, which itself may consist of a number of phases. For example:

- generating ideas;
- working on ideas (e.g. selecting, prioritizing, classifying);
- reshaping and extending ideas (e.g. providing details, critically examining);
- presenting (e.g. preparing a poster).

Planning a discussion by providing a series of preparatory tasks of this kind can help to ensure that, when it comes to whole class discussion, pupils have plenty to say. It can also help build their confidence to contribute.

Reading

The development of pupils' reading is such a vast, complex field that it would be presumptuous – in fact, silly – to seek to cover it here. Instead I will focus on those aspects of reading development that seem to me most salient for lesson planning across the curriculum. In particular, the emphasis in this account will fall on those points most easily overlooked. The 'Further reading' section at the end of this chapter provides references to more broad-based discussions of reading development.

It is easy to assume that in school the status of reading is high. It is, along with (w)riting and (a)rithmetic, one of the three Rs that, it is widely agreed, lie at the centre of the curriculum. The development of literacy is a perennial concern of the education system and one that has attracted a good deal of policy initiatives in recent years.

There are, however, grounds for questioning whether schools prioritize reading development as much as they think they do. Of central importance here is the hidden curriculum – by which I mean the bundle of messages that schools implicitly, and perhaps unwittingly, send to their pupils by means of what the school does rather than what it says.

A key question here is the amount of time devoted to reading: where not much time is devoted to an activity, pupils are likely to conclude it is unimportant. In one school that I taught in a group of colleagues investigated pupils' learning by conducting a series of lesson observations for lessons for one year group across the curriculum. They estimated that the pupils spent about 7 per cent of their time reading. That finding certainly made an impact on me. I am not pretending we can generalize from it statistically – it was one study of one year group, in one school, in one week. The food for thought comes not from the figure but from the divergence from our expectations: we would confidently have said that, as a school, we took reading seriously and placed it at the heart of our curriculum. Had we estimated the percentage, rather than observed it, we would have come up with a very much higher figure. Now imagine walking round your school on a typical day and taking a look into each of the classrooms. What would you expect to see? Is reading a major activity or a minor one?

The question is one of balance, between reading and other modes of language. And, since reading (extended reading, at any rate) rarely happens by accident, balance is a matter of planning. Reading development will be central to the curriculum only if you plan it to be. Note that the question of time is very important – and not only because of its contribution to the hidden curriculum. The amount of time spent on an activity is probably a key determinant in most areas of expertise. In reading, it certainly is. The variables of time spent reading and reading proficiency are strongly related, and causally so. In fact, in reading development positive and negative cycles are observable: pupils who read a lot are more likely to become strong readers; and as their reading becomes more enjoyable and productive, so they tend to go on to read more: so the amount of reading that these pupils do tends to increase each year (at least until high school). Weak readers, in contrast, tend to get into negative cycles: as they develop avoidance techniques, perhaps with the collusion (wittingly or not) of their schools, the amount of reading they do each year falls. If, therefore, you wish to support your pupils' reading development, you need to ensure, no matter what, that your lesson plans allocate time to reading. There's no way round that.

Note that the issue here is not purely one of pupils learning to read. The term I have used above, that is, 'reading development' is deliberately ambiguous: it covers the processes of both learning to read and reading to learn. In some schools, teaching pupils to read may, rightly or wrongly, be seen as the particular province of certain teachers or departments. Developing the capacity to learn, however, is a cross-curricular responsibility – and one that produces benefits across the curriculum too.

Time is not the only component of the hidden curriculum. Another is confidence. If teachers lack confidence in reading as a medium of learning, pupils may well feel the same way. Note that if you are reading this paragraph, you are probably a rarity – someone who believes you can improve professional practice through reading. Sales figures in education publishing suggest that most teachers do not believe that.

The lack of confidence in reading to learn is often evident in teachers' classroom practice. Often written learning resources are restricted to very short texts indeed – a handout consisting of one side of A4, for example. And even then the pupils are often not trusted to learn from the resource through reading it: instead the teacher 'talks through' the sheet so that, in fact, the pupils find there's no real need to read it. (The same is often true of Powerpoint slides.) The routine of 'talking through' can both betoken and transmit a lack of trust in reading as a medium of learning.

A further problem arises when reading invariably leads directly into some form of assessment activity (typically a written exercise). The risk here again lies in the hidden curriculum. Reading may be seen as, at best, insufficient as an educational activity – as if it needs always to be validated by some other activity or, worse, an activity that will always be punished by, say, the drudgery of yet another assessment exercise. The point here is not that reading should never be used in this way: the problem comes when the practice of capping reading with a session of 'real work' becomes routinized.

It is clear that lesson preparation, as we saw in Chapter 8 above, involves decisions over not only the selection of resources but also the way in which they are used during the lesson. It is important to distinguish between the resources themselves and the use to which they are put. We can take here the example of textbooks. Many educators discriminate against textbooks because they are seen as supporting a 'transmission model' of teaching (in which the teacher selects what is to be learnt and attempts to pump that learning into the skulls of pupils whose only role in the process is to be passive, uncritical recipients). Perhaps it is indeed the case that there are teachers who seek to use textbooks in that way. But it does not follow at all that textbooks may be used *only* in that way or that they cannot be combined with other (more active or critical) models of pedagogy. The same holds true for other reading resources.

It is helpful here to have a general model to inform decisions over how written resources may be used. Consider first the relationship between the text and the lesson plan. At one extreme, the teacher may follow a text as a script. For example, where a textbook provides a passage of exposition, the teacher may read it out (or ask the pupils to read it). Then, if this passage is followed in the text by, say, a written exercise, the teacher will duly ask the pupils to complete that exercise. Thus the lesson is shaped by the text in the way a church service is shaped by the liturgy. Alternatively, the teacher may use the text selectively – for example, omitting components of the text, or changing their sequence or perhaps simply selecting a single component (a map or a photograph, for example) for use in the lesson. That is, the teacher may use the text not as a script but as a resource. This distinction provides us with one axis of the model as shown in Figure 11.1:

Script ←——————————————→ Resource

Figure 11.1 Model for use of text: the first axis

Now consider the relationship between the text and the learner. It may be that the learner accesses information from the text and accepts that information – 'takes it in', we may say. For example, the text may say that carbon emissions lead to global warming and the pupil, having read the text, may say something along the lines of 'I've learnt that carbon emissions lead to global warming.' In this case the text is functioning as what we might call a source of learning. Alternatively, however, the text may be held up for examination. The pupil may be encouraged to pose such questions as 'Is this true?,' 'How can we test this?' or 'Are there any alternative views?' When a text is held up for scrutiny like this, we may say that it functions not so much as a source of learning as an object. This distinction provides us with the second axis of our model as shown in Figure 11.2:

Source ◄─────────────────────────────► Object

Figure 11.2 Model for use of text: the second axis

Combining these axes provides us with the model shown in Figure 11.3:

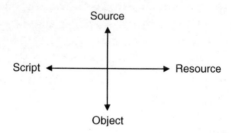

Figure 11.3 Model for use of text: both axes

This model helps to display the choices to be made about how reading resources are used in the classroom. The most important point here is simply that such choices exist. Written resources do not have to be used purely as script or a source. They may be used in the confidence that their use does not commit one to a passive or uncritical pedagogy.

Writing

Classroom writing typically occupies a central position in lesson planning. Unfortunately, writing development does not always receive as much emphasis as the sheer activity of writing. To develop pupils' writing, we need to make room in our planning for developing writing processes as well as for producing outputs.

Writing produced in a single linear process, starting as the opening word of the text is written and ending when the closing word is completed rarely produces pupils' best work. Consider how you can move your pupils on from this 'single sitting' approach to a more graduated one. Adding a subsequent phase for pupils to check their own (or each other's) work can help to improve quality. It enables you to introduce the notion of two distinct writing roles: writer as composer (generating ideas, creating content) and writer as secretary, attending to matters of transcriptions (such as layout and orthography). The composing role may be developed further by introducing an initial phase, devoted to planning.

The really ambitious move is to introduce a phase between composition and checking, in which you ask pupils to improve their writing in ways *other* than checking – by, for example, adding further ideas, rephrasing sentences or changing the sequence of content.

It can help to organize the writing process around two major questions:

- WIIFM? (i.e. 'What's in it for me?').
- WIIFT? (i.e. 'What's in it for them – that is, the readers?').

For example, in the early stages pupils may be allowed to focus on WIIFM? They can ask themselves questions such as 'What do *I* know about this?,' 'What do *I* want to say?' or 'What's *my* best idea?' In later stages you can encourage them to focus on WIIFT by asking questions such as 'Will my reader find this interesting?,' 'Have I told my reader enough about this?' or 'Will the reader get what I mean?'

Of course, pieces of writing do not normally develop in quite the neatly structured, well-organized way that the above notions of 'stages' and 'roles' imply. Yet planning written work in terms of process does provide two major advantages. First, it provides you with an opportunity at each stage to teach the strategies of writing (thereby teaching pupils *how* to write rather than merely 'getting' them to write). Second, it helps to prevent cognitive overload. One of the reasons that pupils – or indeed most of us – find writing difficult is the number and variety of questions buzzing in their heads as they try to write. For example:

- Have I got that idea right?
- How do you spell that word?
- Should I say more about that?
- Where should I put the full stop?
- Have I got my red felt-tip pen?
- Does that make sense?
- How much time have I got?
- What's the word I want there?
- What should the next bit be about?

And so on. Too many ideas of too many types! By planning writing as a series of processes, you can help pupils to focus on different questions at different stages, giving each one due attention without becoming daunted.

Overall, incorporating writing as process, rather than simply as product, into your lesson planning will help you to develop the quality of your pupils' work, as opposed to merely the quantity.

Bringing it all together

At the start of this chapter, I said that it is 'commonly' said that there are four modes of language – 'speaking, listening, reading, writing'. In doing so I wanted to hold open the possibility that there is in fact a fifth mode, namely thinking. At times this mode may be co-extensive with one or more of the first four modes – that is, we may do our thinking through, for example, speaking or writing. But sometimes we don't use any of these four modes: we just sit and think. Ideally our lesson planning should allow room for that mode too.

Though I'm reluctant to reduce the content of this chapter to a single sentence, if I had to, it would be:

Language is a non-transparent learning medium.

Further reading

The taxonomy of listening provided by Andrew Pollard in *Reflective Teaching* is found in the chapter called 'Teaching'. Pam Czerniewksa's example in *Learning about Writing* concerning musical notation comes from the chapter called 'Symbols and Spellings'.

Alan Howe's discussion in *Expanding Horizons* of pair and small group work comes from the chapter called 'Preliminaries'. I strongly recommend trying to obtain a copy of this thoughtful, observant book. As I know to my own benefit, much of Howe's advice is very practical.

Research conducted by educators such as Douglas Barnes and James Britton in the 1970s yielded many rich insights into the relationship between learning and language development. Books such as Barnes, *From Communication to Learning* and *Language, Learner and the School*, and Britton, *Language and Learning* remain highly pertinent – indeed in the current era their insights need to be rediscovered. The same is true of the much maligned government report of the period, *A Language for Life* ('The Bullock Report', 1975), the text of which is available online on Derek Gillard's 'Education in England' website (www.dg.dial.pipex.com).

Frank Smith's books, notably *Understanding Reading*, 6th ed., provide perceptive accounts into the nature of reading and how it should be taught.

Claire Senior, *Getting the Buggers to Read*, provides practical advice.

I have given much more detailed advice on the development of pupils' writing in *100 Ideas for Teaching Writing*. Frank Smith's process-based study, *Writing and the Writer*, is genuinely a classic: it is full of educational insights into the nature of writing.

12

Progression and differentiation

In the introduction to this book I suggested that the planning and preparation stage of teaching could be thought of in terms of a building. First we put in place the four cornerstones – our understanding of:

- Educational aims.
- The needs of stakeholders, especially pupils.
- The context in which we are teaching.
- The cognitive structure of what we teach.

These cornerstones both delimit and support what we do.

Next we construct the first storey – the curriculum. This provides the basis on which we can add the second storey, medium-term planning and the third – short-term planning, including three rooms of particular importance: time, space and language.

Now we need to put a roof on the building. This entails putting two concepts into place: (a) progression and (b) differentiation. I figure these in terms of the building's roof because they are over-arching concepts. They apply throughout and across the curriculum, in every class at every stage.

To understand these two concepts, it may help now to switch metaphors. Think, for a moment, of teaching as an activity that has two dimensions. There is what we might call the vertical axis, namely time. Progression in education is a vertical concept: that is, it is concerned with the order in which we do things and the question of when we do them.

Differentiation, on the other hand, is a horizontal concept. It is concerned with differences, at any particular stage in the curriculum – differences between pupils, differences in the provision we make for them and, crucially, the relationship between these two set of differences.

The point of this chapter is to consider how to take account of these two fundamental concepts.

Progression

This book has discussed at some length the cognitive structure of what we teach (Chapter 5) and the organization of the curriculum (Chapter 6). So far, however, we have said little about the temporal order of our teaching. We've considered what we teach, but not (yet) when to teach it. How should we decide how to sequence the curriculum?

Conventional wisdom exerts much power here. Schools and their teachers often have strong views of what should be taught when. These are not, however, always based on strong reasoning. Sometimes it's merely a case of 'that's when we always do it'. I once discussed this with a man named Peter, whose job it was to inspect English departments in different schools. He told me that he found that English teachers often had very strong views about which books should be taught when, but that these views differed between schools. In one school the teachers might be adamant – or just take for granted – that a certain novel was a 'Year 10 book' (i.e. suitable for 14–15 year olds), while in another school the teachers might be equally certain that it was a 'Year 8 book'. Peter's experience suggests that it is always worth examining why we do things at certain times and whether the sequencing could be different.

> Reflect on a course with which you are familiar. Which components can you identify that might work as well, or even better, if they were taught (a) earlier or (b) later?

In order to decide how to sequence the curriculum, we need to examine the curriculum from the point of view of the learner. The question that matters is not, 'What do we want teach when?' but rather, 'What would make sense to the learners and help them to learn?' How can we help them to move on from one thing to another, both onwards and upwards, building as they do so on previous learning?

To do this, we need to look both forwards and backwards in the curriculum. For a moment, let's stay with the example of English teaching. Suppose we want pupils in one year group to be able to compare characters from two different stories. This poses two challenges: they have not only to understand each of the characters, but also to organize their ideas within a comparative structure (e.g. they may need to learn how to employ phrases such as 'The main similarity' or 'In contrast'). In this case it may well help if at a previous stage in the curriculum the pupils have had some experience of comparative study based on simpler material – a couple of short articles, for example. Thus we might plan backwards, as it were, by deciding to include such an exercise in the scheme of work for the preceding term.

And we can plan forwards too. If, to continue our example, pupils complete a comparative study of two characters from different stories now, what could they move on to later? Perhaps a comparative study of the stories as a whole, including more characters or other aspects such as plot? Perhaps a comparative study of two longer texts?

Again consider a course that you know well. Focus on one component of the course. What could be included earlier in the course to prepare pupils for that component? What could be included later in the course to build on that component?

As always, it helps to integrate our thinking here with our model of the curriculum. That is, it helps to think through the potential continuities not only in terms of subject matter (perhaps the most obvious type), but also in terms of cognitive structure and modes of learning.

How, for example, can we help pupils to build on the declarative knowledge that they have developed? Here it helps to think in terms both of contiguous knowledge and of comparable knowledge – where 'contiguous knowledge' is that which is closely associated with the topic you are planning to teach and 'comparative knowledge' is knowledge of a different but similar topic from which analogies may be drawn.

How too can we help pupils to build on their procedural knowledge – that is, to apply and refine what they have learnt in the form of skills, techniques and methods? And how can they build on the outlooks, judgement and decision-making abilities?

It might help at this point to consider a couple of examples, one negative and one positive. First, the negative. I occasionally used to come across history curricula that were entirely chronological: young pupils began with the study of prehistoric times and as they grew older worked towards the modern day. Such curricula had a certain commonsense quality, perhaps, but I doubt there are many such curricula left today, even in those parts of the education system untouched by national or state curricula. There were many problems, one of which was simply that pupils' approach and understanding matured (one hoped) as they grew older: while it's not difficult to make a case in favour of developing a mature understanding of modern times, it's much harder to argue that one's understanding of earlier times should necessarily be immature!

Second, the positive. I remember reading Fred Inglis's study of children's literature, *The Promise of Happiness*. In the middle of an essay on Lewis Carroll's *Alice in Wonderland*, Inglis wrote that Carroll was an 'accomplished' poet, 'soaked in the rhythms' of 'masters' such as Wordsworth, adding: 'There can hardly be a better introduction to poetry, as Auden noted'. That simple sentence made me reappraise the way I taught literary study. I realized that at each stage of the English curriculum I was trying to teach more sophisticated literature and more sophisticated techniques at the same time – thus maximizing the chances of confusion! I realized that I could instead teach the more sophisticated techniques – analysing poetic metre, for example – using material already known (texts drawn from children's literature) and *then* apply them to the sophisticated 'masters' such as Wordsworth. That is, I could decouple progression in declarative knowledge from progression in procedural knowledge.

We need, then, to integrate our thinking on progression with our model of cognition. We also need to integrate it with what (in Chapter 6) we have termed the third side of our cubic model of the curriculum, that is, learning modes. The question here is, how can we build on our pupils' experience of each mode of learning, helping them to apply and refine those modes? It helps here to look for opportunities both within modes (e.g. within the theoretical mode, moving from basic to advanced theory) and between modes (e.g. applying theoretical learning to case studies).

Two concepts that particularly help here are 'top-down' and 'bottom-up' knowledge. The first occurs when pupils first learn a general concept and then apply it to particulars. For example, in geography pupils might learn the concept 'region' and then use it to help distinguish various regions from each other. In contrast, 'bottom-up' learning involves pupils moving from particular cases to generalized or theoretical knowledge. In biology, for example, they might learn about the characteristics of various species and then move on to consider what the concept 'species' means.

Differentiation

Differentiation is the process of adapting educational activity to suit the diverse needs and characteristics of the learners. We first encountered this concept in relation to context (Chapter 4). We noted there that teaching the same lesson to different pupils results in different experiences and outcomes. Here we should note two corollaries of this fact. First, where this occurs (where, that is, pupils' experiences and learning differ), we have not actually – regardless of our intention – taught the same lesson at all: the lessons have turned out differently. Second, if this is the case, aiming to teach the same lesson in the first place may not necessarily be the best plan: it might be better to differentiate in advance.

The aim in differentiating one's teaching is to optimize the learning of each pupil. That aim is very easy to state, but difficult to achieve in practice. Essentially, there are three ways of proceeding. First, one may differentiate by outcome. The teacher may set the same task for all pupils, who might then produce very different outcomes. That isn't necessarily a bad thing. For example, in art each pupil may be asked to produce a collage from a certain selection of materials. The results may differ wildly. Well, differences in personal style are one of the things that make art fun. The results may differ in level of achievement too (some may be more inventive, composed, etc. than others). That too is not necessarily a problem. It is useful for assessment purposes (this is, after all, how examinations commonly work). And it may be useful developmentally too: the question would be how much the task had done to help each pupil's collage-making abilities develop.

But although differentiation by outcome isn't necessarily a problem, it can be. If some pupils are set a task that is beyond them and they simply flail and fail, that is no good to any one. The pupils don't develop and they become dispirited. It isn't even very useful for the purposes of assessment. (After all, if you were to set a degree-level Mathematics paper to the population at large, most people would score zero – which would reveal nothing.) To rely willy-nilly on differentiation by outcome is less than professional.

The second way to differentiate is by task. That is, one sets different tasks to different pupils based on one's baseline assessment of them. This method clearly has one advantage: it can help the teacher to ensure that each pupil is working in what psychologists call the Zone of Proximal Development (ZPD). 'ZPD' refers to that area of learning that takes pupils beyond what they already know, but within achievable limits. It helps here to think of trying to catch a bus. If you're already at the stop when the bus arrives, you don't need to stretch yourself at all: you just get on. If you're a long way from the stop when you see the bus arrive, you don't bother running: you know it will have pulled off again before you get to the stop. But if you're quite close, well, if you make an effort, you'll just catch it. In that case, as you run for it you are, in effect, moving through your ZPD.

There are, however, disadvantages to differentiating by task. The main problem is that the success of the method depends on the matching of task to pupil, which in turn depends on the accuracy of the teacher's judgement and the baseline assessment on which it is based. If the selection is poor, the classroom will in effect be full of pupils either waiting for buses or realizing they've missed them. In other words, the classroom will be full of the bored and the dispirited.

A third way to differentiate is by support. That is, one can vary the level and means of support that pupils receive. For example, a teacher might set a task such as practising their tennis serves. Some pupils might be able to do that unaided (or by aiding each other). They might know what a good serve is supposed to be like and which parts of their own serves they need to work on. Others might have little or no idea what to do. They would need to receive some additional support, at least to get them underway.

Here educators sometimes use the analogy of scaffolding. Asking pupils to complete a task can be like asking them to climb an object – a tree, say. Some might be able to climb without any scaffolding. Some might need scaffolding to support them throughout. Others might need some at first but then find they can do without.

These, then – differentiation by outcome, by task and by support – are three main ways to differentiate. In most contexts the teacher will probably need to use each of the three at some point. But before we can plan effective differentiation, we need to decide on what grounds we are differentiating.

Consider a course that you have taught or studied. How differentiated would you say the work was? Seek to identify examples of differentiation by:

(a) Outcome.
(b) Support.
(c) Task.
(d) Some combination of the above.

Say 'differentiation' in some staffrooms and someone will quickly start to talk about 'ability'. One common form of differentiation is to design a core task and then two variations on it: an extension task for the 'most able' (or 'bright') and a simplified version for the 'least able' (or 'slow').

If this approach results in three different levels of task being made available, this can have obvious benefits. But there are problems here too, many of them connected to the concept of 'ability'. It seems extraordinary to me how frequently and confidently some teachers pronounce on pupils' 'ability': so-and-so is, we're informed, a 'low-ability pupil' (though strangely there is resistance to defining teachers in the same way!) I have even encountered some teachers who seem to pride themselves on being able to make such judgements, just as some people pride themselves on judging the ability of racehorses (though strangely it is the bookies who seem to profit). Anyone who has had the experience, as I have, of teaching an adult class full of students who had been written off at school and seeing them proceed to gain good grades on advanced level courses, will know to treat such judgements with scepticism.

A moment's reflection will reveal the problems involved. For one thing, when one asks for evidence of a pupil's ability, the answer is usually couched in terms of *attainment* – what they have learned so far, what they scored on a test, what grade they achieved and so on. But attainment isn't the same thing as ability. There may be many factors that explain attainment – absence, motivation, illness, welfare and so on. A pupil who speaks, say, Punjabi but little English might well not do very well in an English language task: does that mean the pupil is 'low-ability'? Treating attainment as an infallible index of ability is just lazy thinking – especially since statements of ability are usually couched in the present tense ('he *is* a high-ability pupil'), while measures of attainment are always in some sense in the past.

Moreover, in most subjects we are concerned with a range of abilities. If, in a cricket game, a pupil shows that she is good at batting but then performs poorly at bowling, has she really moved from being a 'high-ability pupil' to a 'low-ability' one? Would it not be more accurate to say that there are a number of different abilities involved in playing cricket and that her performance varies between them? And is there any subject on the school curriculum that involves just one ability?

We might also ask whether ability is stable. When someone pronounces that a pupil is a 'low-ability pupil' that could mean, grammatically speaking, that the pupil is 'low-ability' *at present*. Pragmatically, however, that is not what the speaker usually means: usually such pronouncements are intended as stable judgements, enabling us to pigeon-hole pupils once and for all. Now if, for example, you were to read my daughter's reports from primary school, you would find that she performed rather poorly in physical education. I don't doubt the accuracy of these reports. Though she hasn't become an outstanding performer in the subject, she has certainly improved. She's opted to study physical education as an examination subject and is expected by her teachers to get a good grade. She has progressed through several ranks at karate. She seems, then, to have become 'more able'!

None of this, we should note, is to deny cognitive differences in our pupils. That would be absurd. The point is rather that we need a richer, more accurate, professional vocabulary – one that includes, as we have seen, 'abilities' (as a plural, measured at particular moments in time, and liable to change) and 'attainment'.

What terms can you suggest, beyond those used previously, for describing cognitive differences between pupils?

I've discussed the notion of 'ability', and the inaccuracy of labelling based on that notion, because in practice a great deal hangs on it. Three problems arise from muddled thinking in this area.

1. It produces inaccurate descriptions – and hence inaccurate judgements – about our pupils. These, in turn, lead to problems when they are used as the basis of differentiation by task or by support.
2. It leads to self-fulfilling prophecies. If, for example, you decide that a pupil is 'low-ability', the following may well result: (a) you don't set tasks that might actually stretch the pupil and

allow them either to develop or display 'ability', (b) you affect the pupil's sense of self-efficacy and their (and everyone else's) expectations.

3. If we allow the notion of ability to dominate our thinking – and the more it is used as a catch-all term, the more it will tend to do so – we will fail to differentiate by other criteria. That is, we will fail to differentiate effectively.

It is time, then, to ask what else we should take account of when planning to differentiate our teaching. Ask this question in staffrooms and a common response – and a helpful one – is 'special needs'. Among educators there's widespread agreement that some pupils do have special needs that require particular kinds of provision. This is not, however, to say that there is straightforward consensus. Opinions differ widely on such questions as:

– What we mean by 'special needs'.
– What counts as a special need.
– How many different types of special need there are.
– What the best ways of catering for special needs are.
– The relationship between special needs (in general) and special *educational* needs (in particular).

This is, therefore, a difficult area in which to generalize. A list of widely accepted needs would include Attention Deficit Hyper-activity Disorder (ADHD), Asperger syndrome, autism, dyslexia, dyspraxia, emotional and behavioural difficulties (EBD), epilepsy, moderate learning difficulties (MLD), impaired hearing, speech disorders, impaired sight and many (other) medical disorders and physical disabilities. In addition, we should recognize that many pupils have *multiple* needs.

Any such list will prove contentious. Experts in the field will, quite reasonably, disagree over the way I have labelled and cate-gorized these needs (shouldn't 'autism' read 'autistic spectrum disorders', for example?). They will also take issue with what I haven't mentioned (what about 'dysphasia', for example?) Imperfect though it may be, such a list does at least serve two purposes. First, it illustrates that the range and diversity of needs is considerable. Second, it reveals something of the state of flux in educational thinking in this area. There is no stable, coherent, taxonomy. Some items appear to be quite precise, others much looser; some are couched in the singular, others in the plural. This taxonomy is likely to continue to change over time.

Because of the range and diversity of needs, the catch-all term 'special educational needs' is of limited use. It is difficult to see what such needs have in common. The term does, however, serve as a useful prompt to continually observe one's pupils, to check their records and to consider what kinds of provision they require, rather than to assume that 'one size fits all.' Indeed in many cases, schools have a statutory duty to make provision for the special needs of their pupils.

It would be, I think, beyond the range of this book to discuss for each specific need the recommended type of provision. That would require a book in itself – and one that I would not be the best person to write. Fortunately, a number of practical, accessible resources providing such specific advice are widely available, some of which are listed in the 'Further reading' section below.

Beyond special needs, there are numerous other factors to take into account when differentiating one's lesson planning. They include, most notably, the cultural, religious and ethnic identity, socio-economic status, gender and language of pupils. Here too, I have decided not to include specific advice regarding each aspect here (again on the grounds that to do so would, I think, require a book in itself). Guidance on other resources that make good this lack is given below.

In the area in which we live there was a scheme by which one could make a donation to charity and, in return, an architect would visit your house. We donated money so that three architects visited us. The upper floor of our house consisted of a landing, three bedrooms and a bathroom. We wanted to see how the space could be used differently to accommodate a fourth bedroom.

Suppose you were teaching a course on architecture and you wanted to include a problem such as this in the course. How could you differentiate the lesson(s)?

> Consider how you could use differentiation by (a) outcome, (b) task and (c) support.
>
> Consider the impact of a range of factors drawn from the following:
>
> - pupils' cognition and prior learning;
> - special educational needs;
> - pupils' identities and the contexts in which they live;
> - pupils' language(s).
>
> Outline two or three contrasting forms of lesson(s) and consider the advantages and disadvantages of each.

Bringing it all together

I have argued that it isn't sufficient just to rely on a 'one size fits all' approach – just pitching up, teaching a lesson and relying on differentiation by outcome. That may be appropriate for particular lessons, but not as a total approach. I have also suggested that an approach that relies simply on supplementing such a lesson with extension material for the 'bright' and support material for the 'slow' doesn't cut the mustard either. We have added into the mix: the need for a more accurate, variegated, dynamic view of pupils' cognitive capacities; special educational needs; and various aspects of pupils' identities and contexts. And at no point have we pretended that this constitutes anything like a complete list of factors bearing on differentiation.

You could be forgiven, therefore, for beginning to feel overwhelmed. You might teach 30 pupils, each of them different in some way. Do you need every time you teach them to design 30 different lessons? There are not enough hours in the day!

It helps here to think of a spectrum of differentiation. On the one hand, we have the 'one size fits all – all the time' approach. At the other end, we have 30 pupils each following their own course of learning. The latter approach is sometimes used, especially when there are resources to support it. But it carries its own problems. It makes collaborative work, discussion, shared experience and so on difficult or impossible. And that each pupil is following his or her own course of study does not in fact guarantee that the work is in fact fully differentiated. Often the differentiation in resources in such lessons is based on quite a narrow range of factors. For example, in some lessons based on 'individualized learning' one finds pupils working through the same resources at different speeds. This may be nothing more than a disguised form of differentiation by outcome. The point to keep hold of here is that there is a range of options between the two extremes of this spectrum. The middle range of the spectrum of differentiation can offer rich pickings.

Let me finish with some reflections on my own experience. Differentiation is an issue that has concerned me a great deal: the more I've thought about teaching, the more it has figured – and the more aware I've become of how my own practice has fallen short. But I have also realized that, in this area at least, perfectionism probably isn't a helpful frame of mind. I suggest that even if you could decide what a *perfectly* differentiated lesson for your class might be, you probably couldn't provide it. If, like me, you find that perfection is beyond you, my suggestion is rather that you aim for proficiency. I've found in any case that often the first few steps in differentiation can carry you quite a long way – not least because when pupils sense you making those steps they are more likely to try to meet you half way.

One final reflection. When I began teaching I certainly approached lesson planning in terms of 'one size fits all.' I then gradually moved into a second phase of approach, where typically I would start by designing a 'one size fits all' lesson and then work out ways of differentiating for particular pupils or groups. Now, when I design any kind of teaching and learning experience, I tend to use a more flexible approach. I first ask myself, 'What are we trying to do here?' and then try to think of a range of ways of getting there. I like this kind of creative approach, but I don't think I could have worked like that when starting out. In teaching, it seems to me, one can't do everything at once.

> Look again at the sample draft scheme of work (Table 7.1) and lesson plan (Table 7.2) in Chapter 7. What suggestions could you make for improving these plans in the light of the discussion in this chapter of (a) progression and (b) differentiation?

Throughout the book I've been reluctant to reduce the purport of a chapter's contents to a single sentence and here I am going to allow myself the luxury of two sentences.

1. Deliberate over the question of what to teach when and, before making a decision, look at the curriculum both forwards and backwards.
2. Differentiate – but in deciding how to differentiate, take care to differentiate between different forms of differentiation.

Further reading

Tim O'Brien and Dennis Guiney, *Differentiation in Teaching and Learning*, provides an overview of the subject.

For books on education for pupils of differing identities, please see the 'Further reading' section of Chapter 3.

For special educational needs, see the practical guides in Continuum's special educational needs series. The guides cover able, gifted and talented pupils (by Janet Bates), ADHD (Fintan O'Regan), autistic spectrum disorders (Sarah Worth), EBD (Roy Howarth), dyslexia (Gavin Reid), dyspraxia (Geoff Brookes), epilepsy (Gill Parkinson), language and communication difficulties (Dimitra Hartas), pro-found and multiple learning difficulties (Corinna Cartwright) and visual needs (Olga Miller).

13

Coda: Assessment

I hope by now it is unsurprising to find a chapter devoted to assessment in this book. As we saw in Chapter 1, the processes of lesson planning and preparation, on the one hand, and assessment, on the other, are – though in one sense at opposite ends of the teaching processes – in fact inter-related. Hence this chapter.

I have drawn on the architectural metaphor of a three-storey house to illustrate the structure of this book's approach to lesson planning and preparation. For approaching assessment, I propose an alternative metaphor, namely that of a cloister of the type that one often finds in the centre of monasteries. As the *OED* explains, cloister consists of a 'covered walk, often round quadrangle with wall on outer & colonnade or windows on inner side'. Often there is grass growing in the central area. Let us take that lawn to represent pupils' learning. Just as in the first two phases of a teacher's work – first, planning and preparing, then teaching the lesson – it is the pupils' learning that is paramount. That is what everything else is *for*. And just as there are usually four walks, one of each side of the cloister, so we will explore four questions concerning assessment. These are the what, why, how and whither of assessment: that is, we will look at what assessment is, why we should do it, how it can be done, and where assessment leads us to. It is apt that the walks in a cloister tend to be open to the central area, since it is through these four aspects of assessment that we observe, and gain access to, pupils' learning.

We sometimes use the word 'cloistered' to mean something like 'secluded' or 'sheltered'. That too is appropriate, up to a point – since a good part of the activities that comprise assessment are conducted away from the hurly-burly of the classroom, often after hours, often indeed in teachers' own homes. But we should also remember that, in a monastery, cloisters can be busy places – places where monks meet or pass one another as they go on their business between different parts of the monastery. That, perhaps, is the happiest part of the metaphor as it is used here – since assessment is a process in which numerous stakeholders, each with their own business and direction, come face to face. They include pupils, teachers, parents, other youth professionals, exam boards, other educational establishments, employers, government and researchers. The assessment cloister is at times a rather busy place.

What?

A distinction is sometimes made between assessment and various associated activities. These include:

- Monitoring.
- Recording.
- Reporting.
- Evaluation.
- Review.
- Development.

To see how such processes feature in the learning journey, consider the following unremarkable sequence of events.

1. Before teaching a class, the teacher looks at records of pupils' achievements to date. The sources of this information might range from the teacher's own knowledge, through data recorded in a mark book, to test and examination scores, qualitative data stored in pupil files and portfolios of pupils' previous work. The teacher uses these records to inform her lesson planning.

2. During the lesson, the pupils complete various learning activities. For example, they might listen to an explanation given by the teacher, perhaps asking themselves whether they understand what is being said. Or they might complete some practical work, wondering as they do so, 'Am I doing this right?'

3. Also during the lesson the teacher might check the pupils' understanding by asking them some questions. Or she might wander around the room, looking at the work they are producing and offering comments ('Your work's definitely improving').

4. The teacher takes in some work at the end of the lesson. Later she sits and marks it. She writes comments for the pupils.

5. At the same time she grades the work . . .

6. . . . and records the marks.

7. After perhaps quite a lengthy sequence of such lessons she writes a report on each pupil to send home to their parents or guardians. Or perhaps she meets them at a parents' evening and refers to the work completed and the grades achieved.

8. Also at the end of a sequence of lessons – forming perhaps a curriculum module – the teacher reflects on the lessons to consider how successful they have been. Perhaps the teacher's manager considers the results achieved as an indication of how the teacher herself is performing – and maybe even refers to this as, say, part of an appraisal process.

9. And at the same time the teacher looks back at the sequence of lessons and draws some conclusions about how the course can be improved next time round.

10. She looks again at the outcomes of the course and considers what conclusions she can draw about how to improve her own professional practice.

11. The teacher implements changes in the course design and in her own practice.

Roughly speaking – though only roughly – we may say that that events (1) to (5) involve assessment: (1) provides an example of baseline assessment; (2) provides an example of self-assessment (of an informal kind); (3) provides an example of informal assessment involving monitoring; (4) and (5) entail marking and grading. Events (6) and (7) take us into the realms of recording and reporting, respectively (whether these are to be regarded as aspects of assessment or activities in addition to assessment is an uninteresting question of semantics!); (8) provides us with an example of evaluation, as do (9) and (10) – though these last two also involve a process of review and (11) provides an example of development.

In *Understanding Assessment*, David Lambert and David Lines define assessment as 'the process of gathering, interpreting, recording and using information about pupils' responses to educational tasks' (p. 4). This definition is in fact broad enough to encompass the first 10 of the previous 11 activities, including those concerned with evaluation. It is this definition that we will use for the purposes of this chapter.

It is evident that assessment forms a regular part of teachers' work. Indeed, in many cases, especially in the secondary sector, schools' annual calendars are organized around such activities – exam leave, reports, parents' evenings and so on. Much energy and time are devoted to these matters, so it is certainly worth ensuring that we deal with them as effectively and skilfully as possible.

Why?

In Chapter 2 I argued that in lesson planning, clarity about aims helps to optimize the design of learning. The same is true of the contribution made by assessment: if we first clarify what we're trying to achieve, we are more likely to design assessment tasks and procedures appropriately.

In *Assessment*, Sonia Jones and Howard Tanner divide the aims of assessment into three types (pp. 3–4). First, there are managerial aims: for example, 'testing the effectiveness of government policies' or 'holding teachers accountable for the progress of their classes'. Second, there are communicative aims: for example, 'providing information to other teachers, educational institutions or employers about individual students' knowledge and skills'.

And finally there are pedagogical aims: for example, 'giving students an appreciation of their achievements and encouraging success' and 'supporting the teaching process by providing feedback to inform future planning'. Given the concerns of this book – lesson planning, from the point of view of the individual professional – we will focus on the pedagogical aims.

For thinking these through, it is helpful to apply another taxonomy, provided by Lambert and Lines (p. 4). They identify four roles for assessment. There is the certification role (' to provide the means for selecting by qualification'), the summative role ('to provide information about the level of pupils' achievements'), the formative role ('to provide feedback to teachers and pupils about progress in order to support future learning') and, finally, the evaluation role. This final role they characterize as providing 'information on which judgements are made concerning the effectiveness or quality of individuals and institutions in the system as a whole'. For all their characteristic clarity, Lambert and Lines are, I think, a little imprecise here. I suggest we need an additional term, between 'individuals' and 'institutions', namely, 'courses'. For example, as a subject leader I decided to remove one course from the curriculum, mainly on the grounds that the standards of achievement were underwhelming. Lambert and Lines could argue that such a use is included within their characterization of 'formative learning' – but I think it is best to reserve that term for the development of learning within a class or course.

Overall, combining Jones and Tanner's taxonomy with Lambert and Lines's, we may say that we are concerned here with the pedagogical aims and, within these, the formative and (to the extent it concerns the individual teacher) evaluative roles of assessment.

The implementation of such assessment is discussed further in the passages headed 'How?' and 'Whither?' below. First, however, a couple of aspects of the concepts require further clarification. First, there is the distinction between formative and summative assessment. This distinction is central to most thinking on assessment. In general, it is pretty clear what is meant by the two terms. Formative assessment is that which, through providing feedback, helps pupils to improve their learning and teachers to improve their teaching. Note that assessment is genuinely formative only if it is acted on in some way (whether by pupils, teachers, or both): in other words, whatever 'feedback' is provided (pupils' work, teacher's comments, etc.) needs then to be treated as 'feedforward'.

Though formative assessment may involve formal procedures (e.g. a classroom test that pupils revise for), it is often informal. It is also often short term. For example, even within the course of a single lesson, a teacher may realize from monitoring the responses of pupils that a certain part of the lesson content hasn't been understood and may therefore decide to go over the material with the class again. Or the teacher may circulate, looking at individuals' work and providing advice (e.g. 'That's a good idea. Go on, write a bit more about that!'). Formative assessment is typically performed frequently – even at times continuously – and repetitively: it may even be so much a part of a teacher's teaching routine that he or she doesn't even think of it as constituting assessment.

Summative assessment, on the other hand, tends to occur less frequently. On each occasion, it aims to provide a snapshot of pupils' attainment at a particular time. Typically, summative assessment happens at the end of a module or course or at the end of a whole phase of education, involves some formal, standardized procedures, and is designed to yield communicable, comparable, information about the level of each pupil's attainment.

Though the distinction between formative and summative assessment sounds very clear, in practice there is a degree of over-lap. For instance, teacher observations of pupils' practical work during a course (which would normally be thought of as purely formative assessment) may sometimes be used to contribute to a final grade (in which case, they then function as summative assessment). Similarly, results achieved by pupils' in examinations at the end of one year (normally thought of as summative assessment) may constitute part of the baseline assessment used to inform the next year's teaching and learning (and so become formative). The distinction between formative and summative assessment, therefore, is not absolute, for it relies in part on the use that is made of the data.

The second area we should clarify concerns diagnostic assessment. This is assessment of individual pupils' learning, designed not only to assess their strengths and weaknesses, but also to help get behind the data and illuminate what kinds of difficulties an individual is experiencing. In some taxonomies of assessment – as opposed to those examined previously – diagnostic assessment is treated as a category in its own right. Though there may be good reasons for this – it is often more intensive and time-consuming and may require specialist knowledge – here it is treated, on the grounds that the purpose of diagnostic assessment is typically to determine what kind of provision is required, as a form of formative assessment.

In *Marking and Assessment of English,* Pauline Chater quotes a subject leader's outline of the purposes of assessment (pp. 6–7). Here I quote from that account selectively. Please note that passages in square brackets in the text below denote places where I have rephrased text in order to make it more contemporary. According to the subject leader, the purposes of assessment are:

   i) To develop and expand work within the limits of the individual child's ability.
  ii) To provide feedback to the pupil; to let him [or her] know how well [their] work is going.
 iii) To identify strengths and weaknesses . . . so that the teacher can plan and guide the pupil in future work.
  iv) To inform parents about their child's progress.
   v) To inform [other teachers and professionals] about the pupil's performance and attitude.
  vi) To select pupils for courses in [future years].
 vii) To inform [end-users, such as employers and tertiary education institutions] about the progress, achievements and attitudes of the pupils. To some extent teachers use assessment to *predict* how a pupil is likely to cope with a job or course.
viii) To get to 'know' the pupil.
  ix) To get the pupil to assess [her- or] himself.

155

If you were the subject leader, what would you like to add to this list?

We have seen that Jones and Tanner divide the purposes of assessment into the following categories:

1. Managerial.
2. Communicative.
3. Pedagogical.

How would you apply this taxonomy to the subject leader's list?

Lambert and Lines categorize the roles of assessment as follows:

1. Certification.
2. Summative.
3. Formative.
4. Evaluative.

How would you apply their taxonomy to the subject leader's list?

How?

In *An Introduction to Assessment*, Patricia Broadfoot, citing another researcher (G. Madaus), argues that in general there are three ways of conducting assessments. Pupils may (a) supply a product, (b) perform an act or (c) select an answer from several options. We should note that this allows educators plenty of scope. In particular, there is no mention of writing as a necessity: though assessment through writing has become the default option in many subjects, there is nothing inherent in the notion of assessment that requires it.

Often the products supplied, acts performed, or answers selected by our pupils are in response to questions that we have posed. The art of questioning is, therefore, an important one. When setting a written exercise or test, I recommend working through the following stages.

1. Clarify the purpose of the assessment. For example, is it primarily for formative or summative purposes? Which learning objectives do you wish to focus on?

2. Distinguish in your mind between open and closed questions and ensure that you use them appropriately. Closed questions have a limited number of (usually brief) answers (typically either 'yes' or 'no'); open questions are more exploratory and permit diversity. For example, 'Do you agree?' is a closed question; 'How far do you agree?' is an open one.

3. Consider the range of interrogatives available (e.g. Who? Whom? What? When? Whence? Whither? Where? Which? How? Why?). Ensure that you do not limit your selection unduly: use as wide a range as is appropriate.

4. Seek to provide a gradation from easy questions to the hard. For example, one may move from 'low-order' questions (e.g. those requiring only straightforward recall) to 'high-order' ones (requiring, for example, application, analysis or evaluation).

5. When you have drafted your questions, review the list. Ask yourself whether you have included sufficient variety. For example, are there (or should there be) questions about both the big picture *and* the detail, similarities *and* differences, and the past, the present *and* the future?

One common form of formative assessment is questioning as part of classroom discussion. Such questioning can help both the teacher to monitor pupils' understanding and pupils to revise and deepen that understanding. There is, however, an art to productive questioning. Much of the earlier advice concerning written questions applies to oral questioning too. Pay particular attention to the distinctions between open and closed questions and between low-order and high-order questions. Closed questions can be useful for injecting pace and for monitoring understanding quickly. However, too often classroom questions are restricted to sequences of closed questions requiring low-order responses: often answering the question becomes a matter of trying to guess what word is in the teacher's head (in which case, why not just tell them?)

Allow time for pupils to consider responses. One commonly quoted convention is the three-second rule (count to three, slowly, before expecting a response). Three seconds is not always enough (my wife tells me she had a teacher who, having asked a good question, would pick up her knitting and work away at it until someone volunteered an answer). And remember to invite questions as well as answers.

> In *Inclusive Mathematics 11–18*, Mike Ollerton and Anne Watson discuss how to extend one's range of questioning in the (secondary) classroom. They write:
>
> > Questions can be based on 'doing mathematics' as sequences of actions, rather than mathematics as various products, such as correct answers or finished written work. For example, students can be asked to think about 'proving' rather than produce proofs; to think about 'equating' rather than solve equations. Another source of questions comes from looking at mathematical structures and guiding exploration of them. Better questions, in terms of developing mathematical thinking, come from asking what can be done next, rather than asking for factual answers (p. 43).
>
> How can this approach be adapted to other subjects or other phases of education? How could it be applied or extended in your own classroom?

Assessment frequently requires marking. Prompt, conscientious, marking of pupils' work is of course essential. On its own, however, it is of limited use. As we noted earlier, assessment becomes formative only when feedback is interpreted as feedforward. For marking to function effectively as formative assessment, we should ensure that pupils receive work back, reflect on the teacher's marking and understand it (or have the opportunity to query it), and draw implications (perhaps in the form of goals or targets) for their future learning. Without explicit attention being given to the business of turning feedback (the teacher's marking) into feedforward, there is a risk that much of the (often very considerable) time spent by the teacher marking work will have been wasted.

There may be occasions where marking very intensively – marking an entire script, in each place against a wide range of assessment objectives – is appropriate or even required practice.

However, there is no reason why this should be the default option for marking and, indeed, there are good reasons for saying that it shouldn't: marking this way is extremely time-consuming and, if pupils regularly receive scripts covered in myriad corrections, can send confusing and even demotivating messages.

There is, therefore, much to be said for focus. One can focus on different learning objectives for different assessment events. One can focus intensively on selected passages of script and less intensively on others. There is much to be said for explaining to pupils which learning objectives will form the focus of your marking. The very act of specifying them may help to re-enforce pupils' understanding of them; by targeting certain objectives pupils may raise their performance in the specified areas – and become more proficient at assessing their own performance; focusing marking on selected objectives may make marking time-efficient; and pupils understanding of your marking, and their response to it in terms of future learning, may be enhanced. It is, however, important to ensure that, over a number of assignments, a range of learning objectives are covered. One also needs to be vigilant, ensuring that one's focus on specific objectives does not become so tight as to prevent one from even noticing any other aspects of the pupils' work. If, for example, a pupil produces work that measures poorly against specified objectives but does contain other kinds of merit, there is no reason why that merit should necessarily not be acknowledged.

Marking frequently involves grading. This is, or at least should be, a matter of judgement. There is nothing inherent in the nature of marking that requires a grade always to be given. (Giving a grade does not guarantee that marking has been done effectively; and marking may sometimes be effective without a grade.) When grades are given, care is needed to ensure that pupils understand what the grades mean and that they attend also to other components of your marking, rather than treating the grade as all important.

There are essentially three methods for awarding grades, namely norm-, criterion-, and self-referencing. Norm-referenced grades show the attainment of the pupil relative to the larger group (e.g. the class or the year group), regardless of absolute levels of attainment. (Thus an A grade implies only that the pupil's

159

attainment is better than most.) Criterion-referenced grades are calibrated: that is, they indicate the attainment of the pupil measured against a pre-articulated set of standards. (Thus an A grade implies the pupil's work meets a demanding set of standards.) Self-referenced grades specify the attainment of the pupil relative to that pupil's previous attainment. Self-referenced grading seeks to show whether a pupil's work has improved, and if so by how much. (Thus a grade is only meaningful if one knows what grade was given previously.) Implicitly, there is some notion of criterion-referencing at play even within norm-, and self-referencing – notions of one piece of work being 'better' or 'worse' (than somebody else's or the pupil's previous work) imply some form of external standard. The long-term trend in education (based on the theory that measures of absolute performance are more informative than measures of relative performance) has been away from norm-referencing towards criterion-referencing. Often teachers will aim for criterion-referencing when it comes to grades but include an element of self-referencing ('I noticed you've improved . . . ') in the verbal comment.

Whither?

As we have seen, formative assessment requires the conversion of feedback into feedforward. There are various mechanisms by which this process may operate.

1. Assessment data may be communicated to pupils, who may then use them to improve their learning. For example, the teacher's marking may indicate an error so that the pupil can avoid making it in future or may provide advice or a new target.
2. Assessment data, communicated to pupils, may enable pupils to improve their ability to assess their own learning, thereby helping them to monitor and improve their work in future.
3. Assessment data, again communicated to pupils, may provide motivation towards further learning. For example, in the course of writing this chapter I have taken time out for a swimming

lesson; my coach at one point complimented me on incorporating more efficient arm movements into my stroke. Did that comment raise my motivation? You bet it did! Here we should insert a rider concerning praise. It is commonly believed that praise is useful for creating a positive cycle, in which good work leads to praise which leads to more good (or even better) work. So, in some circumstances, it does. But praise can prove a disappointingly weak motivator. Indeed, if the pupil is embarrassed, praise may even have a negative effect. Often, *acknowledgement* will motivate pupils more than praise will do (e.g. if my swimming coach were to say, 'Well done! I noticed your arm movements have become more efficient,' it is the second of those two sentences that I hear).

4. Assessment data, provided to teachers (and other professionals, such as learning assistants), may be used to inform decisions over pedagogy. For example, a teacher may use such data to re-design the next course that the pupils are going to follow. Assessments made during the course may even enable the teacher to improve the course even before it is finished.

The foregoing discussion outlines four mechanisms by which assessment data may improve future learning. What additional possible mechanisms can you identify?

In *Assessment*, Jones and Tanner provide a very helpful list of questions to help teachers ensure that they are using assessment formatively. Some of these questions apply to teaching. For example, how often do you:

1. 'Discuss assessment criteria with your class?'
2. 'Use a student's idea to take the lesson in a . . . different direction?'

Some of their questions apply to marking. For example:

3. 'Do your comments advise about the nature of a good answer?'
4. 'Do you give students time to read, reflect and act on your comments when work is returned?'

Some of their questions apply to the use of tests. For example:

5. 'Are your tests timetabled so that errors and misconceptions . . . can be addressed before the end of the module?'
6. 'After the test, do you help your students to set learning tasks for themselves?'

For each of Jones and Tanner's questions, consider which of the four mechanisms are involved.

So far, in responding to the question 'Whither?', we have considered how data about pupils' learning may be used by pupils themselves and by the teacher in order to improve learning in the future. Finally, we now turn to the question of evaluation. Here we consider how teachers may reflect on their own pedagogy, and gather pupils' responses to it, in order to improve the design and provision of courses in future.

In *Developing Your Teaching*, Peter Kahn and Lorraine Walsh consider how teachers may evaluate their own teaching (pp. 53–61). Though they are writing for teachers in higher education, many of their techniques may be transferred to teaching in schools. One such technique is 'assumption hunting'. This involves 'consciously adopting a critically reflective stance towards the underpinnings of your practice'. The aim is to identify the parts of one's practice that one takes for granted and to hold them up for scrutiny. In particular, they recommend seeking to identify 'espoused theories' (theories we tell ourselves we believe in) and 'theories in use' – the theories we actually adopt in the classroom, especially when under pressure. They argue that the gaps between a teacher's 'espoused theories' and their 'theories in use' do not necessarily pose a problem, but that juxtaposing the two 'creates a dynamic for reflection'. One can, for example, consider why the gaps arise, how satisfied one is with them, and how they could be closed.

A second technique advocated by Kahn and Walsh is action planning. This involves developing a set of structured questions to enable you to explore and experiment with change. For example, taking one's teaching as a whole (or more productively, I suggest, one aspect of one's teaching), one can generate a series of questions under each of the following headings – current practice ('What kind of teacher am I now?'), goal ('What kind of teacher do I want to be?'), and process of transition ('How will I get there?'). One's own responses (and indeed those of others you may consult) can then be used to plan a proposed improvement in pedagogy.

A third technique is to keep a reflective journal of one's teaching. This may consist not only of prose, but also of bulleted lists, drawings, diagrams, and so on. Questions may be used as prompts for journal entries. For example: 'What happened? What did I learn from that incident? How have I been able to apply that learning to my practice?'

A fourth technique is what Kahn & Walsh call 'action-oriented goals'. Here you may choose an aspect of your lessons that you wish to investigate further. Kahn and Walsh provide examples such as 'what they have learned from the session; three good things about the class; something they feel is missing from the class; or their reaction to a new aspect'. The teacher then distributes sticky notes and asks pupils to write their comments anonymously and stick the notes in a designated space (e.g. a wall or whiteboard). One can collect the notes subsequently and use them to reflect on how to change one's pedagogy.

An alternative, known as 'traffic lights' is to use sticky notes (preferably coloured ones) to identify which aspects of the course represent red lights (i.e. those the pupils want to call to a halt), which represent amber (i.e. those the pupils feel need keeping an eye on) and which represent green (i.e. the pupils wish to continue). These can then be collected by pupils posting the three types of stickers in three distinct areas.

Similarly, in *How to Design a Training Course*, Peter Taylor suggests some visual methods for collecting feedback from participants (pp. 147–51). The simplest is a five-point moodometer, in which pupils register their impressions of various components of the course on a scale that runs: two grumpies /one grumpy /

neutral face / smiley / two smilies. A slightly more analytic method is to design a large diagram consisting of a series of concentric rings, divided into a number of segments. These segments each represent components of the course. (Examples might include 'homework', 'materials', 'tasks' or 'discussion'.) Pupils each make a cross in each segment – the closer to the centre, the higher the satisfaction. Finally, and perhaps most sophisticated, one may use a graph. The first axis represents 'process', the second 'product'. Pupils each make a cross on the graph to register their satisfaction. For example, a pupil who has not enjoyed the course as a process, but who is nevertheless satisfied with the work they have produced, will make a cross to represent a low rating on one axis and a high rating on the other.

Bringing it all together

In *Enhancing Learning through Formative Assessment and Feedback*, Alastair Irons, citing a group of researchers at Northumbria University, outlines the conditions under which assessment may contribute most to the development of learning. This, writes Irons (p. 27), occurs in learning environments that:

1. emphasize authenticity and complexity in content and methods of assessment rather than the [mere] reproduction of knowledge and reductive assessment;
2. use high-stakes summative assessment [e.g. formal examinations] rigorously but sparingly rather than as the main driver for learning;
3. offer students extensive opportunities to engage in the kinds of tasks that develop and demonstrate their learning, thus building their confidence and capabilities;
4. are rich in feedback derived from formal mechanisms;
5. are rich in informal feedback ideally providing a continuous flow on 'how they are doing';
6. develop students' abilities to direct their own learning, evaluate their own progress and attainments and support the learning of others.

I do like that word 'rich'!

> The specifications for learning environments that support assessment for learning most effectively, relayed by Irons above, are provided for use in higher education. How well do they apply to schools?
>
> What steps could you take to make the learning environment in your classroom as conducive as possible to assessment for learning?

Though I'm reluctant to reduce the content of this chapter to a single sentence, if I had to, it would be:

Think not planning, then teaching and learning, then assessment, but rather *assessment for learning.*

Further reading

Two books provide overviews of assessment that are both concise and practical. They are Sonia Jones and Howard Tanner, *Assessment*, and Lyn Overall and Margaret Sangster, *Assessment*. Both give emphasis to formative assessment. Jones and Tanner include useful chapters on marking, pupil self-assessment, and examinations. Overall and Sangster's book is aimed at primary school teachers. It includes a chapter on record keeping and a particularly good one on strategies of questioning. I think Jones and Tanner's book is a gem.

Two more extended, comprehensive texts are David Lambert and David Lines, *Understanding Assessment* and James H. McMillan, *Classroom Assessment*. The former has its roots in the English education system and the latter in the American, but both include plentiful material of interest to readers beyond their own territories. McMillan includes sections on assessment before and during instruction.

There is a detailed discussion of classroom questioning in the chapter on 'Class and Individual Dialogue' in Andrew Pollard's *Reflective Teaching*.

In *Making Pupil Data Powerful*, Maggie Pringle and Tony Cobb provide a detailed, practical, guide to using assessment data to improve learning.

Appendices

Appendix A: A Cubic Model of the Curriculum

Figure A.1 illustrates the cubic model of the curriculum.

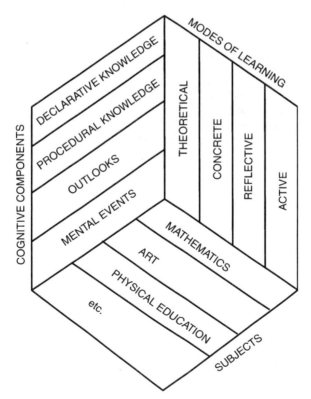

Figure A.1 Cubic model of curriculum

Appendix B: Framework for perfect planning

1. Aims
2. Objectives
3. Assessment data on pupils
4. Scope and content
5. Pedagogical methods
6. Teacher's expectations
7. Learning activities
8. Homework
9. Differentiation of learning
10. Progression in learning
11. Other curricular links
12. Time
13. Space
14. Resources
15. Language
16. Ancillary staff
17. Risks
18. Assessment
19. Evaluation method(s)
20. Review procedure(s)

References

Douglas Barnes, *Language, Learner and the School* (Penguin, 1971).

Douglas Barnes, *From Communication to Curriculum* (Penguin, 1976).

Janet Bates, *Able, Gifted and Talented* (Continuum, 2005).

James Britton, *Language and Learning* (Allen Lane, 1970).

Patricia Broadfoot, *An Introduction to Assessment* (Continuum, 2007) .

Geoff Brookes, *Dyspraxia* (Continuum, 2007).

Graham Butt, *Lesson Planning*, 2nd ed. (Continuum, 2006).

Susan Capel et al., *Learning to Teach in the Secondary School*, 4th ed. (Routledge, 2005).

Corinna Cartwright, *Profound and Multiple Learning Difficulties* (Continuum, 2005).

Pauline Chater, *Marking and Assessment in English* (Methuen, 1984).

Sue Cowley, *Guerilla Guide to Teaching* (Continuum, 2007).

Pam Czerniewksa, *Learning About Writing* (Blackwell, 1992).

Justin Dillon and Meg Maguire, *Becoming a Teacher*, 3rd ed. (Open University Press, 2007).

Fred Fawbert (ed.), *Teaching in Post-compulsory Education*, 2nd ed. (Continuum, 2008).

Andrew Friedman and Sarah Miles, *Stakeholders* (Oxford University Press, 2006).

Heather Fry et al., *A Handbook of Teaching & Learning in Higher Education*, 2nd ed. (Kogan Page, 2002).

Tom Goad, *The First-Time Trainer* (Amacom, 1997).

References

Kathleen Graves, *Designing Language Courses: A Guide for Teachers* (Heinle Elt, 1999).

Kavita Gupta, *A Practical Guide to Needs Assessment* (Jossey-Bass/ Pfeiffer, 1999).

Dimitra Hartas, *Language and Communication Difficulties* (Continuum, 2005).

Nigel Hastings and Karen Chantrey Wood, *Re-Organizing Primary Classroom Learning* (Open University Press, 2002).

Anthony Haynes, *100 Ideas for Lesson Planning* (Continuum, 2007).

Anthony Haynes, *100 Ideas for Teaching Writing* (Continuum, 2007).

Yvonne Hillier, *Reflective Teaching in further and Adult Education*, 2nd ed. (Continuum, 2005).

HMSO, *A language for Life* ('The Bullock Report', HMSO, 1975).

Garry Hornby, *Improving Parental Involvement* (Cassell, 2000).

Roy Howarth, *Emotional and Behavioural Difficulties* (Continuum, 2005).

Alan Howe, *Expanding Horizons* (NATE, 1988).

Fred Inglis, *The Promise of Happiness* (Cambridge University Press, 1981).

Alastair Irons, *Enhancing Learning through Formative Assessment and Feedback* (Routledge, 2008).

Robert Jackson and Eleanor Nesbitt, *Hindu Children in Britain* (Trentham Books, 1992).

Marie Parker Jenkins, *Children of Islam* (Trentham Books, 1995).

Sonia Jones and Howard Tanner, *Assessment*, 2nd ed. (Continuum, 2006).

Peter Kahn and Lorraine Walsh, *Developing Your Teaching* (Routledge, 2006).

Mohamed H. Kahin, *Educating Somali Children in Britain* (Trentham Books, 1997).

K. Paul Kasambira, *Lesson Planning and Class Management* (Longman, 1993).

David Kolb, *Experiential Learning* (Prentice Hall, 1984).

David Lambert and David Lines, *Understanding Assessment* (Routledge, 2000).

Ken Marks, *Traveller Education* (Trentham Books, 2003).

Michael Marland, *Craft of the Classroom* (Heinemann Educational Publishers, 2002).

Roger Marples (ed.), *The Aims of Education* (Routledge, 1999).

Manuel Martinez-Pons, *The Psychology of Teaching and Learning* (Continuum, 2001).

Ian McGrath, *Materials Evaluation and Design for Language Teaching* (Edinburgh University Press, 2002).

Donal McIntyre and Jean Rudduck, *Improving Learning through Consulting Pupils* (Routledge, 2007).

James H. McMillan, *Classroom Assessment*, 2nd ed. (Allyn & Bacon, 2001).

Jay McTighe and Grant Wiggins, *Understanding by Design* (Prentice Hall, 2001).

Jaan Mikk, *Textbook* (Peter Lang, 2000).

Olga Miller, *Visual Needs* (Continuum, 2005).

Kamala Nehaul, *The Schooling of Children of Caribbean Heritage* (Trentham Books, 1996).

David Nunan, *Syllabus Design* (Oxford University Press, 1988).

Mark O'Hara, *Teaching 3–8*, 3rd ed. (Continuum, 2008).

Mike Ollerton and Anne Watson, *Inclusive Mathematics 11–18* (Continuum, 2001).

Fintan O'Regan, *ADHD*, 2nd ed. (Continuum, 2007).

Lyn Overall and Margaret Sangster, *Assessment* (Continuum, 2006).

Lyn Overall and Margaret Sangster, *Primary Teacher's Handbook* (Continuum, 2003).

Gill Parkinson, *Epilepsy* (Continuum, 2006).

Andrew Pollard, *Reflective Teaching*, 3rd ed. (Continuum, 2008).

Maggie Pringle and Tony Cobb, *Making Pupil Data Powerful* (Network Educational Press, 1999).

Gavin Reid, *Dyslexia* (Continuum, 2007).

Jill Rutter, *Supporting Refugee Children in 21st Century Britain* (Trentham Books, 2003).

Farzana Shain, *The Schooling and Identity of Asian Girls* (Trentham Books, 2003).

Janice Skowron, *Powerful Lesson Planning*, 2nd ed. (Corwin Press, 2006).

Frank Smith, *Writing and the Writer* (Heinemann Education Books, 1982).

References

Frank Smith, *Understanding Reading*, 6th ed. (Lawrence Erlbaum, 2004).

Claire Senior, *Getting the Buggers to Read* (Continuum, 2005).

Peter Taylor, *How to Design a Training Course* (Continuum, 2004).

Pat Thomson, *Schooling the Rustbelt Kids* (Trentham Books, 2003).

Decker F. Walker and Jonas F. Soltis, *Curriculum and Aims* (Teachers College Press, 1997).

Leila Walker, *The Essential Guide to Lesson Planning* (Pearson, 2008).

Donna Walker Tileston, *What Every Teacher Should Know About Instructional Planning* (Corwin Press, 2004).

Kevin Wesson, *Sport and PE*, 3rd ed. (Hodder Arnold, 2005).

John West-Burnham, *Managing Quality in Schools: A TQM Approach* (Longman, 1992).

John White, *The Aims of Education Restated* (Routledge & Kegan Paul, 1982).

Robyn Williams, *The Non-designer's Design Book*, 3rd ed. (Peachpit Press, 2008).

Sarah Worth, *Autistic Spectrum Disorders* (Continuum, 2006).

E. C. Wragg, *The Cubic Curriculum* (Routledge, 1997).

Index of names

Index of terms